SKINNY SPICES

SKINNY SPICES

ERICA LEVY KLEIN

Surrey Books

Chicago

SKINNY SPICES is published by Surrey Books, Inc.,
230 E. Ohio St., Suite 120, Chicago, IL 60611.

Second edition: 1 2 3 4 5

This book is manufactured in the United States of America.

Library of Congress Cataloging-in-Publication data:
  Klein, Erica Levy.
    Skinny spices / Erica Levy Klein.
      180 p. cm.
    Includes bibliographical references and index.
    ISBN 0–940625–66–0 (pbk.) : $12.95
     1. Spices. 2. Cookery, International. 3. Low-fat diet–Recipes.
  4. Low-calorie diet–Recipes. I. Title.
TX819.A1K58 1993
641.6'383–dc20   93–19875
                                           CIP

Editorial and production: *Bookcrafters, Inc., Chicago*
Art direction: *Hughes & Co., Chicago*
Cover illustration: *Laurel DiGangi*
Illustrations: *Elizabeth Allen*
Cover photos courtesy American Spice Trade Association and the National Live
  Stock and Meat Board.

For free catalog and prices on quantity purchases, contact Surrey Books at the
address above.

This title is distributed to the trade by Publishers Group West.

Other Titles in the "Skinny" Cookbooks Series:

Skinny Beef   *Skinny Pizzas*
Skinny Chocolate   *Skinny Potatoes*
Skinny Cookies, Cakes, and Sweets   *Skinny Seafood*
Skinny One-Pot Meals   *Skinny Soups*
Skinny Pastas

For Susanna Bensinger

"I end where I began
and know the place for the first time."
—Walt Whitman

Acknowledgments

Special thanks to Susan Schwartz of Surrey Books for her enthusiastic belief that *Skinny Spices* represents a healthy eating trend whose time has come. To Barry Mizes, for his conscientious recipe evaluations and review. And most of all, to my husband, Ken Kroll, who never cared about my weight and made be feel beautiful no matter what the scale said.

CONTENTS

INTRODUCTION

I f I have one quarrel with diet books, it's that the author always portrays herself (or himself) as an example of dieting perfection and implies the rest of us can only experience the same success if we embrace the author's particular eating and fitness regimen. Have you ever noticed how they never seem to endorse anyone *else's* diet and fitness plan? I guess there's just too much ego (and too many dollars) on the line to expect an author to be that objective.

I hope you'll find this a refreshing change of pace, but I refuse to pretend that my Skinny Spice blends are the miracle weight loss cure the world has been waiting for. You can coat yourself in curry powder, dunk yourself in dill, or submerse yourself in cinnamon and you'll still weigh exactly the same unless you're ready to make permanent changes in the way you eat, the way you think about food, and the way you exercise. Making this three-part commitment to a different lifestyle is

1

essential—otherwise you'll just lose the pounds temporarily and gain them all back when you return to eating "normally."

You can take my word for this unfortunate fact. I started out a 215-pound teenager, lost 70 pounds with physician-prescribed diet pills, ate myself back up to 180, Weight Watchered down to 140, high-anxietied up to 185, and then finally lost 55 pounds on Nutri-System (which takes a more behavioral approach to weight loss) and have been a comfortable 130 pounds ever since.

The good news is that spices (and especially the delicious spice blends described in this book) can be a real boon to your weight-loss efforts whether you're trying to slim down on your own or have joined an organized program such as Nutri-System, Weight Watchers, Diet Center, Weight Loss Center, or Jenny Craig. Some of the sweeter blends can even liven up liquid-based diets such as Optifast* and what I call the "poor man's" version—Slim Fast and Ultra Slim Fast.

Why are spices and herbs such excellent diet aids? Because they add next to no calories, fat, or salt to foods, whether they're used individually or in combination. But even more importantly, spices and herbs can make an *incredible flavor difference* in foods that are the staples of any low-calorie diet. I'm talking about the foods that strike fear in every dieter's heart (and stomach)—chicken and turkey . . . fish . . . cottage cheese . . . unbuttered vegetables . . . plain boiled, broiled, and steamed dishes . . . and unsweetened desserts. In short, the foods we usually burn out on long before our weight-loss goals are ever achieved.

With a flavor boost from a *Skinny Spices* homemade spice blend, even low-calorie, low-sodium, low-fat foods can taste more interesting and satisfying. Suddenly, diet choices can go from being punishments (foods to be suffered through and endured) to meals you can actually savor, enjoy, and *live with*—which is one of the real secrets of controlling your weight. And you don't have to cook them; mixing or grinding is all that's necessary.

Just for the record, spices don't have to be "hot" or "tongue tingling." Spices can be cool like my Delicious Dill Blend . . . rich like my Butter Baby Blend . . . sweet like my Choc-o-holic Blend . . . nutty like my Open Sesame Blend . . . or fragrant like my Garlic & Ginger Blend. Just think of them as a miniature "flavor fix" whenever you want to liven up a food you wouldn't normally be able to even look at one more time—much less eat.

Even recent research studies confirm that spice blends like Skinny Spices are a dieter's best friend. A recent study from Canada shows that when you eat a tasty, palatable meal, you burn more calories than eating exactly the same meal in a less flavorful form. Scientists speculate that the sight, smell, and taste of foods we like stimulate our bodies to burn significantly more calories than when we're faced with bland, boring, or unappetizing foods. Still another study, this one from Japan, shows that by including more capsaicin (the "red hot" in red

---

*Consult a doctor before adding any ingredient to Optifast or any other physician-prescribed liquid diet formula.

pepper) in your food, you may be able to fight obesity by increasing your metabolic rate.

Skinny Spices is the first book that looks at spice blends exclusively as a diet aid. It contains more than 50 fast, easy-to-prepare recipes for blends of spices and herbs that will produce mouthwatering gourmet dishes from appetizers and entrees to sweet treats and desserts. I've deliberately kept the spice blends simple (and cooking-free) and the recipes that use them even simpler. That way you can experiment on your own without investing a lot of time and effort in the kitchen. (Frankly, if I see a recipe that has more than five steps, I just flip the page.)

Furthermore, all recipes in *Skinny Spices* have been tested and reviewed for accuracy, then computer-analyzed for calorie, fat, sodium, and cholesterol counts. With a *Skinny Spices* recipe, you always know exactly what you're eating and can then decide how you want to work the dish into your individual diet plan.

As an added bonus, *Skinny Spices* includes tips on mail order sources for both typical and hard-to-find spices, suggestions for handy spice-related gadgets and gizmos, and a list of my favorite brand-name substitutes for high-calorie foods that can help satisfy cravings when you just can't live without that slice of cheesecake or apple pie but don't want the guilt or the calories of the real thing.

I'd enjoy getting your feedback about *Skinny Spices*, and you can feel free to write me in care of the publisher with your questions or comments. In the meantime, I wish you a healthy life that proves "a little spice is always nice."

ERICA LEVY KLEIN

1.
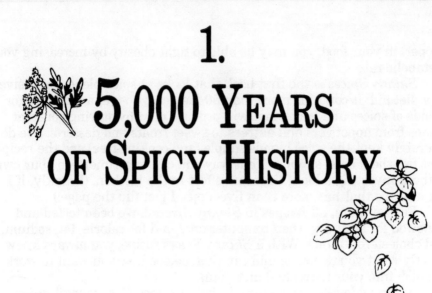
5,000 YEARS OF SPICY HISTORY

G et ready for everything you always wanted to know about spices from the dawn of civilization to the present day. And all in 15 seconds or less!

Spices have always been considered a valuable commodity, and archaeological evidence suggests that spices in one form or another have been selling at a brisk clip for the past 5,000 years. The Egyptians were the first to recognize the value of spices and use them as aromatics and perfumes. Later, when spices became the method of choice for food preservation, their sea-going cousins, the Phoenicians, traded spices for salt and tin along Europe's Mediterranean coast. But it was really the Arabs who were the most successful in opening up spice trade routes throughout the Muslim and Roman empires, and in a relatively short amount of time (historically speaking), they dominated the world's spice trade.

After the fall of Rome, the Venetians took their turn at trying to gain control of the world's highly lucrative spice trade routes. But

4

eventually even these merchants of Venice found themselves sharing their routes with ships from Portugal, Spain, Holland, and England.

The plantations that eventually sprang up as a result in colonies throughout the New World assured that spices were no longer controlled by any one country. Today, spices arrive in our supermarkets and gourmet shops from every part of the tropics, and demand is so high that spices are often the mainstay of an entire country's economy.

Did you get all that? Great! There'll be a quiz on Monday. But in the meantime, you've just earned an honorary DOS degree—Doctorate of Spice-ology!

2.
GETTING THE SKINNY ON SKINNY SPICES

Are Skinny Spices really all that skinny when it comes to calories? Happily, the answer is yes. Most spices and seasonings weigh in at between 3 and 10 calories a level teaspoon, according to the American Spice Trade Association. (C'mon, would they lie, I ask you?)

Since most recipes require only ⅛ to ½ teaspoon of a particular spice or spice blend, and that amount is usually divided among six or eight portions, you can quickly see why spices are a dieter's best friend. Spices are also incredibly low in fat, protein, carbohydrates, and sodium, making them ideal for medically restricted or special diets.

Here's a brief overview of calorie counts for various spices:

- **Seasonings with 5 calories or less per teaspoon:**

basil	rosemary
bay leaf	sage
garlic powder	savory
marjoram	tarragon
parsley flakes	thyme

6

- **Seasonings with 6 to 10 calories per teaspoon:**

allspice	ginger
caraway seed	mace
cardamon	dry mustard
cinnamon	onion powder
clove	oregano
coriander	paprika
cumin	pepper, all types
dill	sesame seeds
fennel	turmeric

- **Seasonings with under 15 calories per teaspoon:**
  celery seeds
  nutmeg
  poppy seeds

3.
PREPARATION AND STORAGE TIPS

One beauty of the spice blends that follow is that you just have to mix them—no cooking is necessary. It's that simple! But to bring out the best in your spices, try these helpful tips, courtesy of Barbara Gibbons, "The Slim Gourmet." Barbara is also the author of *Light and Spicy*, a marvelous low-calorie, spice cookbook:

- Try marinating or heating herbs in oil to bring out their deepest flavors.
- Enhance the flavor of seeds such as poppy and sesame by toasting in a regular oven or toaster oven.
- Keep spices in a cool, clean, dry place out of the sunlight to prevent evaporation of oils and flavor.
- Keep containers tightly closed after each use.
- Use ground spices within a year to take advantage of best flavor. (Whole spices keep their flavor almost indefinitely and may be

purchased in larger amounts.) Herbs tend to lose flavor a little faster than spices, so you may want to use them up sooner.

- To preserve herbs, either freeze or dry them. Before either process, wash and dry herbs well. *To freeze:* spread in a single layer on a baking sheet in the freezer. After herbs are completely frozen, pack them up in small freezer bags. Use frozen herbs in soups, stews, and hot dishes or defrost for use in salads and cold foods. *To dry:* in the microwave, lay herbs on a sheet of paper toweling and cook for several minutes on high. In the oven, scatter herbs on a baking sheet in a slow oven with the door open, watching carefully to see that they don't get crisp.

4.
Not the Same Old Grind: Spicy Gadgets & Gizmos

D epending on the ingredients in a *Skinny Spices* blend (and whether you prefer powdery or coarsely ground spice blends), you may want to process your herbs and spices for a few seconds in a *blender, coffee grinder,* or *food processor.* Of course, you can also resort to the old fashioned method and use a *mortar and pestle* along with plenty of elbow grease. But lazy spice blender that I am, I always prefer to use a high-tech timesaver.

These days, I use a *blender* to achieve the consistency I want with many of my own homemade blends—especially combinations that contain peppercorns, nutmeg, stick cinnamon, or whole coriander. If you don't happen to own a blender, grinder or processor, you can crush these spices by placing them between two sheets of wax paper (or in a baggie) and flattening them with a rolling pin. However, a blender offers an added advantage in that it can uniformly mix a spice blend in a way that's difficult to achieve any other way.

10

I've also had great success with the Pepper Mate, an all white, space-age pepper mill that looks like a child's oversized wind-up toy. A special acrylic compartment at the bottom of the device catches the freshly ground spices. Another good alternative is the hand-held spice grinder set from The Spice Merchant, a mail order firm that specializes in Asian spices, condiments, and foodstuffs. The set includes six empty jars, each with its own grinder and acrylic storage container. The Spice Merchant's address is listed in the "Your Mail Order Guide to Spices" in the back of the book, but I'll also repeat it here:

The Spice Merchant
P.O. Box 524
Jackson Hole, WY 83001
(307) 733-7811

Another alternative to these techniques is to use a *food processor*, but generally, you're compelled to make bigger batches of the spice blend before this appliance is really effective, and it's dangerously easy to overprocess and turn your spice blend into a spice paste. Although this is not a major disaster, *Skinny Spice* blends are simply more distinctive—and more eye-appealing—when the spices retain their original form.

All of the spices and herbs used in the following recipes are in their dried form. If you want to use fresh equivalents, the ratio is ⅓ to ½ teaspoon of dried = 1 tablespoon of fresh. It's best to begin with more conservative amounts of herbs and spices and add more according to your taste.

5.

SPICES FROM A TO Z

I magine yourself strolling slowly through a fragrant garden filled with every spice and herb from around the world and this is just a sample of what you'd find:

allspice—its scent reminiscent of cinnamon, cloves, and nutmeg, "all" rolled into one.

anise—a sweet, licorice-like taste that's terrific with vegetables, stews, and soups.

basil—sweet and pungent; great in tomato sauce or combined with oregano and garlic in Italian dishes.

bay leaf—a strong taste that stands up to poultry, fish, sauces, and stews.

caraway—with a mild, tangy quality that's similar to dill seed.

cardamon—sharp, pungent, and sweet with a cinnamon-like aroma.

cayenne pepper—a tongue-searing red pepper that adds a lively kick to "tame" foods.

celery seed—celery-like flavor that zips up tuna, coleslaw, and salad dressings.

chervil leaf—a strong, herbal taste with just a hint of tarragon. The perfect complement for fish, vegetables, and salads.

chives—the mild onion taste that's wonderful heaped generously onto salads, soups, and plain-baked potatoes.

cilantro—dried coriander leaf with an exotic parsley-like flavor that livens up poultry, vegetables, and sauces.

cinnamon—sweet, fragrant, and versatile enough to spice up everything from desserts and drinks to beef and chicken.

cloves—a type of evergreen bud typically found in spiced drinks, marinades, glazes, and sweet treats.

coriander—spicy and citrus-like. Great for chili, stir-frys, and coleslaw.

cumin—the major flavor ingredient in most chili powders. Especially good on meats and in yogurt-based dishes.

dill weed—the feathery leaf of the dill plant, with a pungent kick and a light, heady fragrance.

fennel seed—sweet, licorice-like seeds similar to anise but a lot milder in taste. A lovely addition to pork, fish, or seafood dishes.

fenugreek—spicy, slightly bitter maple-like flavor that is usually found in curry mixtures.

garlic—adds a dazzling, pungent flavor and fragrance to any dish. New varieties will even leave your breath smelling sweet!

ginger—a sharp, spicy-sweet fragrance that's perfect for adding a taste of the Orient.

horseradish—a white root with a hot, hearty flavor.

mace—the ground outer covering of nutmeg, with a more compelling, pungent fragrance.

marjoram—a milder cousin of oregano.

mint—light, fragrant, and comforting. Peppermint is the more biting variety; spearmint is a lot milder.

mustard—hot and spicy; a devilish addition to salad dressings, eggs, and vegetable dishes.

nutmeg—mild, nutty, distinctive, and fragrant. Great in sweets or in sauces.

oregano—the dominant herb in many spaghetti sauces, and just as terrific with tomatoes, peppers, zucchini, eggplant, and dips.

paprika—a mild, ground reddish pepper that's delicious with chicken, eggs, and dressings.

parsley—the ever-present garnish, with an herbal flavor that's great in soups, stews, sauces, and salad dressings.

pepper—a spicy berry found in three familiar forms: black, green, and white.

poppy seed—tiny seeds with a sweetish, nutty taste and texture.

rosemary–fragrant, strongly flavored leaf that looks like a miniature pine needle. The ultimate herb for chicken.

saffron–the most expensive of all spices, a traditional accompaniment to many Indian, Spanish, and Mediterranean dishes.

sage–strong, pleasant flavor with a sweet, herbal fragrance.

savory–a mild, thyme-like taste that adds special fragrance to meats and fish.

sesame seed–mild, nut-like flavor and a pleasant, toasted quality.

tarragon leaf–a rich, sweet flavor and fragrance faintly reminiscent of anise.

thyme–distinctive, pleasant herbal flavor and fragrance that's wonderful with seafood, tomato-based sauces, or in salad dressings.

turmeric–a brilliant yellow ground spice with a peppery aroma and a ginger-like flavor. Adds the golden color to curry powder.

6.
A QUICK GUIDE TO MEASUREMENTS AND SWEETENER EQUIVALENTS

- **General Measurements**

3 teaspoons	= 1 Tablespoon
1 Tablespoon	= ½ fluid ounce
4 Tablespoons	= ¼ cup
8 Tablespoons	= ½ cup
1 cup	= ½ pint
2 cups	= 1 pint
4 cups	= 1 quart
4 quarts	= 1 gallon
8 ounces	= ½ pound
16 ounces	= 1 pound

- **Dry Sweetener Approximate* Equivalents**

1 packet	= 2 teaspoons sugar
3 packets	= 2 Tablespoons sugar
6 packets	= ¼ cup sugar
12 packets	= ½ cup sugar
25 packets	= 1 full cup sugar

- **Liquid Sweetener Approximate* Equivalents**

⅛ teaspoon liquid	= 1 teaspoon sugar
¼ teaspoon liquid	= 2 teaspoons sugar
½ teaspoon liquid	= 4 teaspoons sugar
¾ teaspoon liquid	= 6 teaspoons sugar
1 teaspoon liquid	= 8 teaspoons sugar
1½ teaspoons liquid	= ⅓ cup sugar
1 Tablespoon liquid	= ½ cup sugar
2 Tablespoons liquid	= 1 cup sugar

*Most sweeteners vary in sweetness according to the brand. For best results, check the label, add a minimum of sweetener, and then increase to taste.

7.

A SPRINKLE OF WORDS ABOUT SALT SUBSTITUTES

Because sodium can lead to water retention, which can be extremely frustrating when you're trying to lose weight, I've used "salt substitute" wherever I thought salt would add extra flavor in a recipe or a spice blend. However, some people just don't care for the taste of pure salt substitutes (potassium chloride) and prefer a blend of salt substitute and real salt. These products are usually labeled "Lite," and the label usually indicates that this is a salt substitute containing at least some of the real thing (sodium chloride).

If you have no problems with water retention as a result of sodium, you may even prefer to go ahead and use regular salt. Whether you use salt substitutes or the real McCoy, salt lightly to begin with and then slowly add more according to your taste. You can always increase the saltiness of foods, but it's difficult to perform a salt-ectomy once it's already been included.

8.

ALL-AMERICAN SPICE & HERB BLENDS

Butter Baby Blend
Garlic Lover's Herb Blend
Lemon Herb Blend
Mild Garlic & Parsley Blend
Pseudo Seasoned Salt Blend I
Pseudo Seasoned Salt Blend II
Classic Pepper Quartet Blend
Vegetable Blend
Fish Hater's Blend
Seafood Blend
Poultry Blend
Cottage Cheese Blend
Onion Pepper Blend
Delicious Dill Blend
Meat Blends

BUTTER BABY BLEND

5 Tablespoons Butter Buds or Molly
  McButter Sprinkles
½ teaspoon salt substitute
1 Tablespoon dried parsley

Skinny Spices Tip

When you don't have the fresh herbs called for in a recipe but you do
have the dried version, add a Tablespoon of chopped fresh parsley to
each teaspoon of the dried herbs for an excellent substitute.

Smooth as Butter Spread

Yield: 16 servings

- 8 ounces ricotta or farmer cheese
- 4 Tablespoons skim milk
- 2–3 Tablespoons **Butter Baby Blend** (to taste)

Blend all ingredients together in a mixing bowl until smooth and creamy. Refrigerate.

Nutritional Data

PER SERVING				EXCHANGES			
Calories:	24	Cholesterol (mg):	4.5	Milk: 0.0		Bread: 0.0	
Fat (gm):	1.1	Sodium (mg):	31	Veg.: 0.0		Meat: 0.2	
Sat. fat (gm):	.7	% Calories from fat:	42	Fruit: 0.0		Fat: 0.1	

Butterball Veggies

Yield: 2 servings

- ⅓ cup coarsely chopped celery
- 8 ounces fresh or frozen peas
- ½ teaspoon thyme leaves
- 2 teaspoons **Butter Baby Blend**
  Additional salt substitute to taste

In a tightly covered saucepan, cook the celery in ½ cup of water over medium heat for 5 minutes or just until tender. Add peas, cover the saucepan, and cook for 8 to 10 minutes more before draining well. Sprinkle peas with thyme and salt; toss with Butter Baby Blend until thoroughly moistened.

Nutritional Data

PER SERVING				EXCHANGES			
Calories:	99	Cholesterol (mg):	0	Milk: 0.0		Bread: 1.2	
Fat (gm):	.4	Sodium (mg):	136	Veg.: 0.1		Meat: 0.0	
Sat. fat (gm):	.1	% Calories from fat:	3	Fruit: 0.0		Fat: 0.0	

GARLIC LOVER'S HERB BLEND

3 Tablespoons garlic granules or powder
1½ Tablespoons toasted sesame seeds
½ Tablespoon onion powder
1½ Tablespoons paprika
½ Tablespoon dried orange peel
½ teaspoon dried ground red pepper

Skinny Spices Tip

This suggestion is courtesy of Joe Cahn, founder of the New Orleans
School of Cooking. To make a no-fat thickening agent, sprinkle flour on
a shallow, non-stick cookie tin or baking pan and slow-bake in the oven
at 325° for 1 hour. Use this "roux" to thicken soups or stews by
combining with a *double* amount of cold water, and whisk it smooth or
shake in a jar. Slowly whisk this mixture into a simmering soup or stew;
it will thicken once it reaches 180°.

VAMPIRE CHASER'S CREAMY DRESSING

Yield: 1 cup (16 servings)

½ cup low-fat cottage cheese
½ cup low-fat buttermilk
½ lemon, peeled and seeded
4 chopped radishes
½ chopped green pepper
1 teaspoon salt substitute
¼ teaspoon **Garlic Lover's Herb Blend**
Dash paprika

Place cottage cheese, buttermilk, and lemon in food processor or blender. Process or blend at high speed until smooth and velvety. Add all remaining ingredients, and pulse or blend at high speed until mixture is creamy and free of lumps.

Nutritional Data

PER SERVING				EXCHANGES			
Calories:	10	Cholesterol (mg):	.6	Milk: 0.0		Bread:	0.0
Fat (gm):	.2	Sodium (mg):	37.1	Veg.: 0.0		Meat:	0.1
Sat. fat (gm):	.1	% Calories from fat:	14	Fruit: 0.0		Fat:	0.0

SUBLIMELY GARLICKY CRAB CAKES

Yield: 3 servings

6 ounces canned or frozen crabmeat
3 slices toasted bread
3 soft boiled eggs
Onion powder to taste
⅛ teaspoon **Garlic Lover's Herb Blend**
⅛ teaspoon dehydrated onion flakes
Dash pepper
Parsley flakes and paprika to taste
¼ cup low-sodium chicken bouillon

Crumble toast and mix with eggs and chicken bouillon. Then mix with all other ingredients and divide into three custard-type baking dishes. Bake at 350° for 20 minutes.

Nutritional Data

PER SERVING				EXCHANGES			
Calories:	213	Cholesterol (mg):	270	Milk: 0.0		Bread:	1.0
Fat (gm):	7.3	Sodium (mg):	300	Veg.: 0.0		Meat:	2.3
Sat. fat (gm):	2	% Calories from fat:	32	Fruit: 0.0		Fat:	0.5

LEMON HERB BLEND

2 Tablespoons dried lemon peel
1 Tablespoon dried basil
½ Tablespoon ground thyme
½ Tablespoon ground oregano
½ Tablespoon paprika
½ Tablespoon toasted sesame seeds
2 teaspoons parsley flakes
1 teaspoon celery seed
1 teaspoon onion flakes
1 teaspoon garlic powder or granules
1 teaspoon cayenne pepper

Skinny Spices Tip

For more flavor with less fat, use a teaspoon of sesame seed paste (tahini) to enliven homemade, low-fat, low-calorie salad dressings.

WISCONSIN CHEESE LOG

Yield: 8 servings

- 4 ounces sharp Cheddar cheese, shredded
- ⅓ cup part-skim ricotta cheese
- 1 Tablespoon plus 1 teaspoon dry white wine
- ¼ teaspoon **Lemon Herb Blend**
  Garlic powder to taste
  Onion powder to taste
  Salt substitute to taste
- ¼ cup minced fresh parsley

In blender or food processor, combine cheeses, Lemon Herb Blend, wine, garlic powder, onion powder, salt substitute and process until smooth. In the center of a sheet of plastic wrap, sprinkle 2 Tablespoons parsley, and then spoon the cheese mixture over the parsley in a line. Now sprinkle the remaining 2 Tablespoons of parsley over cheese, and enclose the cheese in wrap, forming a log about 6 inches long by 2 inches wide. Transfer to the freezer and let freeze for about 20 minutes; turn log over and freeze until firm, 10 to 25 minutes longer. To serve, remove plastic wrap and surround with Melba rounds.

Nutritional Data

PER SERVING				EXCHANGES			
Calories:	73	Cholesterol (mg):	18.1	Milk: 0.0		Bread:	0.0
Fat (gm):	5.5	Sodium (mg):	101	Veg.: 0.0		Meat:	0.7
Sat. fat (gm):	3.5	% Calories from fat:	68	Fruit: 0.0		Fat:	0.8

DECADENT VEAL CHOPS

Yield: 6 chops

- 6 loin veal chops
  Salt substitute to taste
- 10 ounces low sodium beef bouillon or consomme
- 2 teaspoons **Lemon Herb Blend**
- 1 Tablespoon Worcestershire sauce
- ½ chopped green pepper
- ½ cup chopped black olives
- ½ chopped onion
- ¼ chopped pimento

Sprinkle chops with salt substitute and Lemon Herb Blend. Brown on both sides under the broiler. Transfer chops to skillet and add all remaining ingredients. Now cover and simmer 40–45 minutes until veal is tender.

Nutritional Data

PER CHOP				EXCHANGES			
Calories:	259	Cholesterol (mg):	94.4	Milk:	0.0	Bread:	0.0
Fat (gm):	16	Sodium (mg):	369	Veg.:	0.2	Meat:	3.3
Sat. fat (gm):	5.7	% Calories from fat:	56	Fruit:	0.0	Fat:	1.4

MILD GARLIC & PARSLEY BLEND

6 Tablespoons parsley flakes
2 teaspoons garlic powder or granules
1 teaspoon onion flakes
1 teaspoon paprika
1 teaspoon finely ground black pepper

Skinny Spices Tip

For a tomato sauce with a Turkish accent, combine no-salt-added tomato sauce with bits of onion, garlic, hot pepper, cumin, cinnamon, black pepper, and parsley. Add olive oil to taste. Serve with grilled poultry or lamb.

DEVILED FISH SALAD

Yield: 6 servings

½ cup plain low-fat yogurt
½ cup chili sauce
32 ounces cooked white fish (halibut, sole, haddock, etc.)
½ teaspoon **Mild Garlic & Parsley Blend**
Lettuce
Pimento

Blend well yogurt, chili sauce, and Mild Garlic & Parsley Blend. Toss gently with flaked fish. Serve on "cupped" lettuce leaves garnished with pimento.

Nutritional Data

PER SERVING				EXCHANGES			
Calories:	229	Cholesterol (mg):	63.3	Milk: 0.1		Bread: 0.0
Fat (gm):	4.9	Sodium (mg):	124	Veg.: 0.2		Meat: 3.9
Sat. fat (gm):	.9	% Calories from fat:	20	Fruit: 0.0		Fat: 0.0

GARLIC TOAST

Yield: 2 servings

2 slices of 40-calorie white or wheat bread
1 Tablespoon soft diet margarine
½ teaspoon **Mild Garlic & Parsley Blend**

Brush bread with margarine. Sprinkle liberally with Mild Garlic & Parsley Blend. Slice bread in strips lengthwise. Bake in 350° oven for 10 minutes. Makes 8 "fingers" of garlic toast.

Nutritional Data

PER SERVING				EXCHANGES			
Calories:	57	Cholesterol (mg):	0	Milk: 0.0		Bread: 0.5
Fat (gm):	1.9	Sodium (mg):	110	Veg.: 0.0		Meat: 0.0
Sat. fat (gm):	.4	% Calories from fat:	28	Fruit: 0.0		Fat: 0.3

Pseudo Seasoned Salt Blend I

1 Tablespoon mustard powder
1 Tablespoon garlic powder
2 teaspoons parsley
2 teaspoons dill weed*
2 teaspoons onion powder
2 teaspoons savory
2 teaspoons ground thyme
2 teaspoons paprika
2 teaspoons white pepper
1 teaspoon dried lemon peel*

Skinny Spices Tip

For a lean and lovely "cream" sauce base, combine 2 cups of part-skim ricotta cheese, ¼ cup cake flour, and 2 Tablespoons of fresh low-fat milk. Combine all ingredients in food processor or blender. Use by the Tablespoon as a low-calorie thickener for soups, sauces, stews, and other dishes. Approximately 20 calories per Tablespoon.

Pseudo Seasoned Salt Blend II

2 Tablespoons garlic powder
2 teaspoons ground basil
2 teaspoons ground marjoram
2 teaspoons ground thyme
2 teaspoons parsley flakes
2 teaspoons ground savory
2 teaspoons ground mace
2 teaspoons onion powder
2 teaspoons finely ground black pepper
2 teaspoons ground sage
1 teaspoon cayenne pepper

CHESAPEAKE BAY OYSTER STEW

Yield: 4 servings

1 pint shucked oysters
12 ounces clam juice
½ teaspoon of *either* **Pseudo Seasoned Salt Blend**
¼ teaspoon celery seed
Pepper to taste
2 cups skimmed milk
1 Tablespoon saltless diet margarine
1 teaspoon Worcestershire sauce
1 Tablespoon cornstarch
4 ounces canned water chestnuts, diced

Combine oysters and clam juice in the top of a double boiler and heat the mixture, but do not boil. Add Pseudo Seasoned Salt Blend, pepper and celery seed. Add milk, margarine, and Worcestershire sauce, but be careful not to allow the mixture to boil. Dissolve cornstarch in cold water and add to stew, cooking until thickened. Serve with water chestnuts as a low-calorie substitute for oyster crackers.

Nutritional Data

PER SERVING				EXCHANGES			
Calories:	201	Cholesterol (mg):	67.7	Milk: 0.5		Bread: 0.4	
Fat (gm):	4.8	Sodium (mg):	694	Veg.: 0.5		Meat: 1.3	
Sat. fat (gm):	1.3	% Calories from fat:	21	Fruit: 0.7		Fat: 0.3	

SUPREMELY SATISFYING VEGETABLES

Yield: 8 servings

1 Tablespoon canola oil
1 cup diagonally sliced carrots
1 cup sliced cauliflower
½ cup sliced celery
½ cup sliced green pepper
¼ cup diced onion

  ¾ cup water
1 can bamboo shoots
1 cup fresh or canned water-pack pineapple
   chunks
2 Tablespoons low-sodium soy sauce
½ teaspoon of *either* **Pseudo Seasoned Salt
   Blend**
2 teaspoons cornstarch

Saute all vegetables in heated oil until coated and shiny (a wok is ideal but a frying pan will do nicely). Add water; cover and simmer for 10 minutes. Add bamboo shoots and pineapple. Mix together all remaining ingredients and stir into vegetables. Cook and stir until sauce begins to thicken, about 2–3 minutes.

◆

Nutritional Data

PER SERVING				EXCHANGES			
Calories:	43	Cholesterol (mg):	0	Milk:	0.0	Bread:	0.0
Fat (gm):	1.9	Sodium (mg):	31.3	Veg.:	1.0	Meat:	0.0
Sat. fat (gm):	.2	% Calories from fat:	36	Fruit:	0.0	Fat:	0.3

◆

Classic Pepper Quartet Blend

2 Tablespoons coarsely ground black pepper
2 Tablespoons finely ground white pepper
2 Tablespoons finely ground green or pink pepper
1 Tablespoon finely ground cayenne pepper

Skinny Spices Tip

For a tasty, economical alternative to ordinary hamburgers, try patties made from low-calorie ground veal. A food processor fitted with a steel blade quickly and easily does the job, or you can use a meat grinder. Start with veal cubes and add any of the following during processing: a clove of garlic, a few fresh basic leaves, a squirt of lemon, or a pinch of nutmeg.

THICK AND JUICY HAMBURGERS

Yield: 6 burgers

1½ pounds extra lean ground beef
1½ teaspoons salt substitute
1½ teaspoons **Classic Pepper Quartet Blend**
1 Tablespoon freshly grated onion
1 teaspoon dried dill weed
¼ cup red wine

Mix beef together with all other ingredients and wine. Let the combination sit in the refrigerator for at least an hour to thoroughly combine flavors. Shape the meat into 6 patties, and broil or barbecue for 5 minutes on each side. Serve with tomato, onion, pickle, or your favorite hamburger garnish on a low-calorie whole-wheat bun.

Nutritional Data

PER BURGER				EXCHANGES			
Calories:	308	Cholesterol (mg):	112	Milk: 0.0		Bread: 0.0	
Fat (gm):	18	Sodium (mg):	93.5	Veg.: 0.0		Meat: 4.0	
Sat. fat (gm):	7	% Calories from fat:	54	Fruit: 0.0		Fat: 1.5	

CHINESE RESTAURANT SWEET-AND-SOUR CHICKEN

Yield: 4 servings

1 fryer (2 pounds) cut up, with skin removed
½ cup wine vinegar
½ cup low-sodium soy sauce
2 cloves garlic, crushed
½ teaspoon **Classic Pepper Quartet Blend**
½ teaspoon salt substitute
1 teaspoon prepared mustard
¼ cup ketchup
2 Tablespoons honey
½ cup low-sodium chicken bouillon

Place chicken in 2-quart casserole and cover with sauce made from all remaining ingredients. Cover and bake at 325° for ½ hour until juicy and tender.

Nutritional Data

PER SERVING				EXCHANGES			
Calories:	325	Cholesterol (mg):	131	Milk: 0.0		Bread: 0.0	
Fat (gm):	3.1	Sodium (mg):	500	Veg.: 0.1		Meat: 5.8	
Sat. fat (gm):	.8	% Calories from fat:	9	Fruit: 0.8		Fat: 0.0	

VEGETABLE BLEND

1½ Tablespoons onion powder
1½ Tablespoons toasted sesame seeds
1 Tablespoon dried chives
1 Tablespoon dried tarragon
½ Tablespoon dry mustard
½ Tablespoon dill weed
1½ Tablespoon dried red bell pepper
flakes
½ Tablespoon salt substitute

Skinny Spices Tip

To liven up green beans, add any of the following skinny spices to melted diet margarine: marjoram, lemon juice, nutmeg, dill seed, dehydrated onion, curry, or basil.

GARDEN FRESH VEGETABLE SPREAD

Yield: 1 cup (16 servings)

⅔ cup creamed low-fat cottage cheese
¼ cup minced green pepper
2 Tablespoons chopped pimento
Pepper to taste
1½–2 teaspoons **Vegetable Blend** to taste

Mix all ingredients well in blender or food processor, and use as a dip for veggies or as a spread on Melba toast, pitas, or low-calorie bread.

Nutritional Data

PER SERVING				EXCHANGES			
Calories:	8	Cholesterol (mg):	.4	Milk:	0.0	Bread:	0.0
Fat (gm):	.1	Sodium (mg):	38.5	Veg.:	0.0	Meat:	0.2
Sat. fat (gm):	.1	% Calories from fat:	13	Fruit:	0.0	Fat:	0.0

SQUASH BISCUITS

Yield: 8 servings

1 12-ounce package frozen cooked squash
1 egg
1 teaspoon **Vegetable Blend**
1 Tablespoon flour
1 teaspoon low-sodium baking powder

Defrost squash and drain well, patting completely dry with paper towel. Combine the squash with egg, flour, Vegetable Blend, and baking powder. Drop this mixture by heaping tablespoons onto a heated, non-stick frying pan (it also helps to coat it with non-stick spray) and heat until brown. Turn biscuits over to brown the other side.

Nutritional Data

PER SERVING				EXCHANGES			
Calories:	30	Cholesterol (mg):	26.5	Milk:	0.0	Bread:	0.4
Fat (gm):	.7	Sodium (mg):	9.1	Veg.:	0.0	Meat:	0.1
Sat. fat (gm):	.2	% Calories from fat:	19	Fruit:	0.0	Fat:	0.1

FISH HATER'S BLEND

1 Tablespoon savory
1 Tablespoon thyme
1 Tablespoon fennel
1 Tablespoon sage
1 Tablespoon marjoram
1 Tablespoon bay leaf
½ Tablespoon dried chives
½ Tablespoon dehydrated onion

Skinny Spices Tip

For an easy, light sauce to accompany a low-calorie fish dish, combine
½ cup salt-free diet margarine, 2 teaspoons grated lemon rind, and 3
Tablespoons lemon juice.

CRABMEAT NAMED DESIRE

Yield: 4 servings

1 10-ounce package frozen cauliflower
1 10-ounce package frozen spinach
1 teaspoon low-sodium chicken bouillon powder
  or granules
½ cup skim milk
½ teaspoon minced garlic
½ teaspoon **Fish Hater's Blend**
  Salt substitute to taste
  Pepper to taste
2 7-ounce cans crabmeat
1 Tablespoon grated Parmesan cheese
  Paprika to taste

Cook cauliflower and spinach as directed on packages and drain well. Combine cauliflower, bouillon, skim milk, garlic, Fish Hater's Blend, salt, and pepper in blender and blend until smooth. Combine with spinach and crabmeat in 1-quart casserole. Sprinkle with cheese and paprika. Bake at 375° for 12–15 minutes or until golden.

Nutritional Data

PER SERVING				EXCHANGES			
Calories:	140	Cholesterol (mg):	100	Milk:	0.0	Bread:	0.0
Fat (gm):	2.5	Sodium (mg):	556	Veg.:	1.5	Meat:	2.3
Sat. fat (gm):	.6	% Calories from fat:	16	Fruit:	0.0	Fat:	0.0

COUNTRY RANCH DRESSING

Yield: 1 cup (16 servings)

1 cup buttermilk
1 packet low-sodium chicken bouillon
2 Tablespoons **Fish Hater's Blend**

Mix all ingredients together and chill.

Nutritional Data

PER SERVING				EXCHANGES			
Calories:	7	Cholesterol (mg):	.5	Milk:	0.1	Bread:	0.0
Fat (gm):	.2	Sodium (mg):	60	Veg.:	0.0	Meat:	0.0
Sat. fat (gm):	.1	% Calories from fat:	21	Fruit:	0.0	Fat:	0.0

SEAFOOD BLEND

2 Tablespoons toasted sesame seeds
2 Tablespoons dill weed
2 Tablespoons paprika
1 Tablespoon garlic powder

Skinny Spices Tip

Experiment with spices that bring out the best in fish and seafood: basil, bay, chives, curry, dill, fennel, garlic, ginger, mustard, oregano, parsley, savory, and tarragon.

Richer Than Rich Chilled Shrimp Soup

Yield: 4 cups

½ lb. cooked and peeled shrimp
1 large cucumber, peeled and diced
1 large tomato, seeded and diced
1 quart buttermilk
   Salt substitute to taste
   Pepper to taste
   Dash of Tabasco sauce
   Dash of Worcestershire sauce
1 Tablespoon **Seafood Blend**

Mix together all ingredients in blender until smooth. Chill 24 hours and serve garnished with fresh dill or parsley.

Nutritional Data

PER CUP				EXCHANGES			
Calories:	171	Cholesterol (mg):	119	Milk:	1.1	Bread:	0.0
Fat (gm):	3	Sodium (mg):	388	Veg.:	0.6	Meat:	1.0
Sat. fat (gm):	1.5	% Calories from fat:	16	Fruit:	0.0	Fat:	0.0

Velvety Tuna Casserole

Yield: 1 serving

2 ounces regular or hickory-smoked flaked tuna
   (water packed)
2 ounces farmer cheese
1 teaspoon canned or fresh mushrooms
1 teaspoon green pepper
1 teaspoon pimento
½ teaspoon **Seafood Blend**
   Paprika

Season farmer cheese with Seafood Blend. Add tuna and remaining ingredients and place in baking dish. Sprinkle top with paprika. Bake at 350° for 20 to 30 minutes until crusty on top.

Nutritional Data

PER SERVING				EXCHANGES			
Calories:	166	Cholesterol (mg):	56.4	Milk:	0.0	Bread:	0.0
Fat (gm):	8	Sodium (mg):	389	Veg.:	0.1	Meat:	2.9
Sat. fat (gm):	2.3	% Calories from fat:	44	Fruit:	0.0	Fat:	0.4

POULTRY BLEND

2½ Tablespoons sage
2½ Tablespoons thyme
2 Tablespoons marjoram

Skinny Spices Tip

For a spicy Latin American chicken marinade, combine equal parts orange and grapefruit juice plus ½ teaspoon grated grapefruit rind. Place chicken in a glass bowl, add juice and rind mixture, 2 mashed garlic cloves, and a generous pinch of cumin seeds or ground cumin. Cover and refrigerate for several hours before broiling or barbecuing.

SEXY SIREN'S CHICKEN

Yield: 4 servings

¼ cup low-sodium soy sauce
  Juice of 1 lemon
1 teaspoon **Poultry Blend**
¼ teaspoon pepper
1 teaspoon dried ground ginger
2 lbs. chicken, cut up and skin removed
10 ounces thawed Chinese vegetables
4 ounces small cocktail onions

Combine all ingredients except vegetables and onions and pour over chicken. Let steep for 30 minutes or more. Brown chicken under broiler, basting it liberally with sauce. Transfer chicken to casserole, add Chinese vegetables, drained onions, and remaining marinade. Cover and bake in 350° oven for about 45 minutes or until tender.

Nutritional Data

PER SERVING				EXCHANGES			
Calories:	303	Cholesterol (mg):	131	Milk: 0.0		Bread: 0.0	
Fat (gm):	3	Sodium (mg):	580	Veg.: 1.9		Meat: 5.8	
Sat. fat (gm):	.8	% Calories from fat:	9	Fruit: 0.1		Fat: 0.0	

TANGY LIME & HERB TURKEY

Yield: 8 servings

3 pounds of turkey pieces
  Marinade:
1 cup tomato juice
½ cup reconstituted lime juice
⅛ teaspoon **Poultry Blend**
2 Tablespoons minced onion or dehydrated
  equivalent
2 teaspoons tarragon
1 teaspoon salt substitute
½ teaspoon hot sauce

Coat turkey in marinade and refrigerate for approximately 2 hours, turning occasionally. Bake in 400° oven for 45 minutes, basting with sauce.

Nutritional Data

PER SERVING				EXCHANGES			
Calories:	328	Cholesterol (mg):	145	Milk: 0.0		Bread: 0.0	
Fat (gm):	12.4	Sodium (mg):	246	Veg.: 0.4		Meat: 5.8	
Sat. fat (gm):	4.1	% Calories from fat:	35	Fruit: 0.1		Fat: 0.0	

COTTAGE CHEESE BLEND

2 Tablespoons dried chives
2 Tablespoons parsley flakes
1 Tablespoon celery seed
1 Tablespoon garlic powder
1 Tablespoon chervil

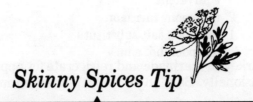

Skinny Spices Tip

An easy and tasty method for testing herb and spice combinations is to mix several herbs and spices into separate portions of light cream cheese or low-fat ricotta. After allowing the mixtures to sit at room temperature for one hour, spread on vegetables or Melba toast rounds, noting which flavors you like and which ones seem overpowering. Adjust seasonings until you discover exactly the right "formula," and write down all ingredients and measurements for future reference.

BLUE RIBBON COTTAGE CHEESE DIP

Yield: 8 servings

- ½ cup low-fat cottage cheese
- ½ teaspoon minced fresh onion
- 1 Tablespoon lemon or lime juice
- ½ teaspoon **Cottage Cheese Blend**
  Dash of substitute salt
  Dash of freshly ground pepper

Puree cottage cheese until smooth in food processor or blender. Combine all remaining ingredients and chill well.

Nutritional Data

PER SERVING				EXCHANGES			
Calories:	11	Cholesterol (mg):	.6	Milk: 0.0		Bread: 0.0	
Fat (gm):	.1	Sodium (mg):	57.4	Veg.: 0.0		Meat: 0.2	
Sat. fat (gm):	.1	% Calories from fat:	12	Fruit: 0.0		Fat: 0.0	

EGG-STATIC EGG SALAD

Yield: 1 serving

- 1 hard boiled egg, finely chopped
- 1 Tablespoon celery, chopped
- ½ teaspoon dehydrated onions to taste
- ⅛ teaspoon **Cottage Cheese Blend**
- ⅓ cup low-fat cottage cheese

Mix all ingredients well and serve on lettuce.

Nutritional Data

PER SERVING				EXCHANGES			
Calories:	134	Cholesterol (mg):	215	Milk: 0.0		Bread: 0.0	
Fat (gm):	6.1	Sodium (mg):	372	Veg.: 0.1		Meat: 2.3	
Sat. fat (gm):	2.1	% Calories from fat:	42	Fruit: 0.0		Fat: 0.5	

ONION PEPPER BLEND

3 Tablespoons dried onion
2 Tablespoons coarsely ground black pepper
2 Tablespoons parsley flakes

Skinny Spices Tip

Did you know that eating raw peppers in food can reduce the chance of heart disease and aid circulation by increasing the production of fibrinolysin (a blood clot dissolver) in the blood? This keeps your blood flowing smoothly—and the increase in fibrinolysin can follow within 30 minutes of eating a pepper. That includes the mild varieties!

ONIONY OVEN FRENCH FRIES

Yield: 4 servings

2 medium potatoes
2 Tablespoons canola oil
1 teaspoon **Onion Pepper Blend**

Scrub potatoes but do not peel. Cut into wedges and place in a bowl of cold water for 15 to 20 minutes. Drain and pat dry with paper towels. Put wedges into a plastic bag and add salad oil. Shake to coat wedges lightly. Sprinkle Onion Pepper Blend over all surfaces of the "fries." On a non-stick cookie tin prepared with cooking spray, arrange potato wedges in a single layer. Bake in a preheated 500° oven for 12 to 15 minutes until potatoes are crisp and browned outside. Season to taste with salt substitute and paprika.

Nutritional Data

PER SERVING				EXCHANGES			
Calories:	133	Cholesterol (mg):	0	Milk:	0.0	Bread:	1.0
Fat (gm):	6.9	Sodium (mg):	3.9	Veg.:	0.0	Meat:	0.0
Sat. fat (gm):	.5	% Calories from fat:	46	Fruit:	0.0	Fat:	1.3

MUSHROOMS EXTRAORDINAIRE

Yield: 24 mushroom caps

24 fresh mushrooms (approx. 1 lb.)
½ cup chopped parsley
1 4-ounce can mushrooms, stems and pieces, finely chopped
2 Tablespoons minced fresh onion
2 Tablespoons powdered low-sodium chicken bouillon
¼ teaspoon **Onion Pepper Blend**
¼ cup water

Remove stems from fresh mushrooms and boil caps until tender. Chop reserved stems finely and add to remaining ingredients. Heat the mixture in a non-stick pan until tender. Stuff this mixture into mushroom caps, and spread them evenly on a cookie sheet. Bake at 375° for 20 minutes.

Nutritional Data

PER MUSHROOM CAP				EXCHANGES			
Calories:	8	Cholesterol (mg):	.1	Milk:	0.0	Bread:	0.0
Fat (gm):	.2	Sodium (mg):	45	Veg.:	0.3	Meat:	0.0
Sat. fat (gm):	0	% Calories from fat:	17	Fruit:	0.0	Fat:	0.0

DELICIOUS DILL BLEND

2 Tablespoons dill
2 Tablespoons onion flakes
1 Tablespoon garlic powder
1 Tablespoon toasted sesame seeds
½ Tablespoon dried lemon peel
½ teaspoon dried cayenne pepper (optional)

Skinny Spices Tip

Use dill leaf rather than dill seed in cold, uncooked dishes since dill flavor is released more quickly from the leaf than from the seed.

LUSCIOUS YOGURT DIP

Yield: 8 servings

8 ounces plain yogurt
1 raw cucumber unpeeled, finely chopped
1 medium clove of garlic, minced
½ teaspoon **Delicious Dill Blend**
Paprika

Pat cucumber dry in paper towel. Then combine with remaining ingredients and refrigerate for several hours to combine flavors. Sprinkle with paprika and use as a dip for fresh veggies or as a cool topping for a hot baked potato.

Nutritional Data

PER SERVING				EXCHANGES			
Calories:	23	Cholesterol (mg):	1.7	Milk: 0.2		Bread: 0.0
Fat (gm):	.5	Sodium (mg):	20.7	Veg.: 0.2		Meat: 0.0
Sat. fat (gm):	.3	% Calories from fat:	18	Fruit: 0.0		Fat: 0.1

DILLIGHTFUL CARROTS

Yield: 4 servings

1 Tablespoon soft diet margarine
½ teaspoon **Delicious Dill Blend**
½ cup dry white wine
2 teaspoons minced onion
½ cup low-sodium chicken bouillon
2 teaspoons cornstarch
2 drops hot pepper sauce
3 cups hot, cooked sliced carrots

Melt margarine in saucepan; add Delicious Dill Blend, wine, and onion. Combine bouillon with cornstarch. Add to the contents of the pan, along with hot pepper sauce. Cook, stirring over moderate heat until sauce thickens. Add carrots, lower heat, and simmer 5 minutes.

Nutritional Data

PER SERVING				EXCHANGES			
Calories:	92	Cholesterol (mg):	0	Milk: 0.0		Bread: 0.1
Fat (gm):	1.6	Sodium (mg):	150	Veg.: 1.6		Meat: 0.0
Sat. fat (gm):	.3	% Calories from fat:	15	Fruit: 0.0		Fat: 0.7

MEAT BLEND I

2 Tablespoons rosemary
2 Tablespoons savory
1 Tablespoon thyme
1 Tablespoon marjoram

MEAT BLEND II

1 Tablespoon black pepper
1 Tablespoon garlic powder or granules
1 Tablespoon onion powder
1 Tablespoon chili powder
½ Tablespoon dried lemon peel
½ Tablespoon mustard seed
½ Tablespoon allspice
½ Tablespoon coriander
½ Tablespoon marjoram
½ Tablespoon oregano

Skinny Spices Tip

Avoid sugary barbecue sauces whenever possible. Instead, choose fruit juice or no-salt-added tomato juice to baste meats. You can add extra flavor with fresh herbs or liquid smoke seasoning.

SHEPHERD'S PIE

Yield: 6 wedges

8 ounces extra lean ground beef round
1 teaspoon of *either* **Meat Blend**
5 Tablespoons skim milk
1 cup biscuit mix
1 small onion, chopped
½ cup finely minced green bell pepper
2 tomatoes, peeled and diced
½ teaspoon oregano
½ teaspoon ground cumin
3 Tablespoons low-calorie mayonnaise
½ cup plain low-fat yogurt
½ cup shredded part-skim mozzarella cheese

Spread meat in a shallow layer on a broiler pan and brown under the broiler. Drain and discard all fat. Break meat into chunks and season with Meat Blend. Prepare non-stick pie pan by coating with cooking spray. Using two forks or a pastry blender, cut milk into biscuit mix until a soft dough forms. Spread dough in bottom and up the sides of pan. Put the browned beef in the bottom of the pie and sprinkle with onion, green pepper, tomatoes, oregano, and cumin. Blend mayonnaise with yogurt and spoon over top of pie; sprinkle with shredded mozzarella. Bake in preheated 375° oven for 30 minutes. Remove from oven and wait 5 to 10 minutes before slicing pie into six wedges.

Nutritional Data

PER WEDGE				EXCHANGES			
Calories:	300	Cholesterol (mg):	47.3	Milk:	0.2	Bread:	1.1
Fat (gm):	14.1	Sodium (mg):	503	Veg.:	0.5	Meat:	1.7
Sat. fat (gm):	4.9	% Calories from fat:	43	Fruit:	0.0	Fat:	1.6

52

STICK-TO-YOUR-RIBS VEGETARIAN STEW

Yield: 4 servings

- 9 ounces uncooked lentils
- 1 quart water
- 12 ounces pared potatoes, diced
- 1 cup diced onions
- 1 cup diced celery
- 1 cup diced carrots
- ¼ cup chopped fresh parsley
- 4 packets low-sodium beef broth and seasoning mix
- 2 teaspoons of *either* **Meat Blend**
- 1 bay leaf
- ⅛ teaspoon ground cumin

In 4-quart saucepan, combine lentils and water and bring to a rolling boil. Reduce heat to medium, cover pan, and let simmer on low heat for several hours until lentils are tender. Add remaining ingredients to lentils and stir to combine; cover and cook over low heat until potatoes are tender: 45 minutes to 1 hour. Remove bay leaf before serving.

Nutritional Data

PER SERVING				EXCHANGES			
Calories:	339	Cholesterol (mg):	0	Milk:	0.0	Bread:	3.6
Fat (gm):	.9	Sodium (mg):	300	Veg.:	1.5	Meat:	0.2
Sat. fat (gm):	.1	% Calories from fat:	2	Fruit:	0.0	Fat:	0.0

9.

SALAD
SPICE
BLENDS

◆

Tangy Tarragon & Herb Blend
St. Tropez Salad Topping Blends

◆

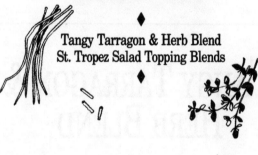

TANGY TARRAGON & HERB BLEND

1 Tablespoon tarragon
1 Tablespoon thyme
1 Tablespoon onion powder
1 Tablespoon dry mustard powder
1 Tablespoon coarsely ground black
  or red pepper
1 Tablespoon fennel
1 Tablespoon savory

Skinny Spices Tip

To make a kinder, gentler vinegar, half fill a bottle with crushed raspberries, strawberries, or other berries, then cover the fruit with wine vinegar. Refrigerate for 1 to 2 weeks, then strain. Refrigerate again and use in salads or for sauteing or stir-frying chicken or fish.

Summer Pasta Salad

◆

Yield: 4 servings

2 cups cooked spinach elbow macaroni, chilled
1 cup cooked cut green beans, chilled
1 medium tomato, chopped
1 ounce herb cheese (any type)
2 Tablespoons low-calorie mayonnaise
¼ cup plain low-fat yogurt
¼ teaspoon **Tangy Tarragon & Herb Blend**
  Dash garlic powder
  Dash freshly ground pepper

Combine macaroni, green beans, tomato; set aside. In small mixing bowl, using a fork, mash together cheese and mayonnaise until cheese is completely blended; stir in yogurt, Tangy Tarragon & Herb Blend, garlic powder, and pepper. Pour this dressing over macaroni mixture and toss well to combine.

◆

Nutritional Data

PER SERVING				EXCHANGES			
Calories:	157	Cholesterol (mg):	7.5	Milk:	0.1	Bread:	1.3
Fat (gm):	3	Sodium (mg):	148	Veg.:	0.7	Meat:	0.3
Sat. fat (gm):	1.6	% Calories from fat:	17	Fruit:	0.1	Fat:	0.3

Herbed Superb Artichokes

◆

Yield: 8 servings

2 10-ounce packages frozen artichoke hearts
½ cup water
1 Tablespoon olive oil
2 Tablespoons white wine
1 Tablespoon lemon juice
½ teaspoon salt substitute
4 peppercorns
1 bay leaf
1 clove garlic, crushed
½ teaspoon **Tangy Tarragon & Herb Blend**

Combine all ingredients and simmer for 5 minutes until artichoke hearts are tender. Remove artichokes. Cook liquid uncovered for 10 minutes to reduce it. Strain liquid over artichokes. Chill for several hours or overnight. Serve cold.

◆

Nutritional Data

PER SERVING				EXCHANGES			
Calories:	50	Cholesterol (mg):	0	Milk:	0.0	Bread:	0.0
Fat (gm):	2	Sodium (mg):	37.7	Veg.:	1.2	Meat:	0.0
Sat. fat (gm):	.3	% Calories from fat:	33	Fruit:	0.0	Fat:	0.4

St. Tropez Salad Topping Blend I

1½ Tablespoons dried chives
1½ Tablespoons chervil
1½ Tablespoons parsley
1½ Tablespoons basil
1 Tablespoon celery seed

Skinny Spices Tip

Wondering what to do with chervil? Use it with fish, macaroni, potato
and Caesar salads, or coleslaw. Or try adding it to low-calorie
mayonnaise for use on sandwiches or in deviled eggs.

St. Tropez Salad Topping Blend II

1 Tablespoon savory
1 Tablespoon garlic
1 Tablespoon oregano
1 Tablespoon basil
1 Tablespoon thyme
1 Tablespoon marjoram
½ Tablespoon finely ground black or cayenne pepper
½ Tablespoon paprika

Skinny Spices Tip

Use thyme as a fragrant complement to meats, poultry, seafood, tomatoes, tomato-based sauces, salad dressings, marinades, and bastes.

String Bikini Beans

Yield: 6 servings

1 onion, chopped
1 clove garlic, minced
1 teaspoon canola oil
1 teaspoon of *either* **St. Tropez Salad Topping Blend**
1 tomato, peeled and diced
1 Tablespoon minced green pepper
1 Tablespoon minced celery
1 Tablespoon chopped parsley
1 Tablespoon dry white wine
  Salt substitute
  Pepper
1 pound string beans, cooked

Saute onion and garlic in oil until lightly browned. Add all remaining ingredients except beans. Simmer for 10 minutes. Pour sauce over cooked beans and mix well.

Nutritional Data

PER SERVING				EXCHANGES			
Calories:	18	Cholesterol (mg):	0	Milk:	0.0	Bread:	0.0
Fat (gm):	.9	Sodium (mg):	3.8	Veg.:	0.3	Meat:	0.0
Sat. fat (gm):	.1	% Calories from fat:	40	Fruit:	0.0	Fat:	0.2

Cold and Luscious Riviera Soup

Yield: 2 servings

2 cups buttermilk
1 medium cucumber
1 packet low-sodium chicken bouillon
2 teaspoons dehydrated onion flakes
1 teaspoon dried dill weed
½ teaspoon of *either* **St. Tropez Salad Topping Blend**
1 teaspoon salt substitute
2 sprigs parsley

Peel and dice cold cucumber. Measure 2 cups buttermilk and pour into blender. Add all the other ingredients plus diced cucumbers. Blend for 3 minutes at medium speed. Taste and correct seasoning. Serve immediately in mugs or soup bowls. Garnish with parsley.

Nutritional Data

PER SERVING				EXCHANGES			
Calories:	120	Cholesterol (mg):	8.6	Milk:	1.1	Bread:	0.0
Fat (gm):	2.4	Sodium (mg):	385	Veg.:	0.7	Meat:	0.0
Sat. fat (gm):	1.4	% Calories from fat:	17	Fruit:	0.0	Fat:	0.0

10.

FRENCH SPICE BLENDS

♦

Provence Blend
Hearty Mustard Blend
Gallic Herbes Blend

♦

PROVENCE BLEND

2 Tablespoons rosemary
2 Tablespoons thyme
1 Tablespoon savory
1 Tablespoon fennel
1 Tablespoon basil

Skinny Spices Tip

Rosemary can add a crowning touch to roast chicken, pork, shellfish, vegetables, and citrus fruit salads.

TOTALLY INEBRIATED CHICKEN

Yield: 4 servings

1 fryer (2 lbs.), cut up and skin removed
1 cup canned tomatoes with liquid
½ cup white wine
1 clove garlic, minced
¾ teaspoon **Provence Blend**

Combine all ingredients and pour over chicken in shallow pan. Bake uncovered at 325° for 1½ hours. Baste frequently.

Nutritional Data

PER SERVING				EXCHANGES			
Calories:	281	Cholesterol (mg):	131	Milk:	0.0	Bread:	0.0
Fat (gm):	3	Sodium (mg):	247	Veg.:	0.5	Meat:	5.8
Sat. fat (gm):	.8	% Calories from fat:	10	Fruit:	0.0	Fat:	0.4

ULTIMATE EGGPLANT

Yield: 6 servings

1 Tablespoon olive oil
1 eggplant, peeled and diced
2 cloves garlic, minced
1 green pepper, diced
3 tomatoes, skinned and diced
½ pound fresh mushrooms, sliced
1 teaspoon salt substitute
2 teaspoons **Provence Blend**

Heat olive oil in skillet or wok and saute eggplant and garlic until lightly browned. Add remaining ingredients, including Provence Blend, and simmer, uncovered, 10 minutes until eggplant is tender.

Nutritional Data

PER SERVING				EXCHANGES			
Calories:	58	Cholesterol (mg):	0	Milk:	0.0	Bread:	0.0
Fat (gm):	2.7	Sodium (mg):	9.1	Veg.:	1.5	Meat:	0.0
Sat. fat (gm):	.4	% Calories from fat:	37	Fruit:	0.0	Fat:	0.4

HEARTY MUSTARD BLEND

2 Tablespoons dry mustard
2 Tablespoons mustard seed
2 Tablespoons parsley flakes
½ Tablespoon salt substitute
½ Tablespoon black pepper

Skinny Spices Tip

For a robust, creamy hollandaise sauce, combine 1 cup of buttermilk, 1 teaspoon lemon juice, sugar substitute to taste, ¼ teaspoon salt substitute, and ½ teaspoon **Hearty Mustard Blend.** Mix well and refrigerate before serving over fish or steamed vegetables.

Golden Temptation Chicken

Yield: 4 servings

1 fryer (2 pounds), quartered, skin removed
½ teaspoon curry powder
½ teaspoon **Hearty Mustard Blend**
1 Tablespoon honey
½ teaspoon grated orange rind
½ cup orange juice
½ teaspoon salt substitute
    Dash pepper
2 oranges, peeled and sliced

Sprinkle chicken with curry powder and Hearty Mustard Blend, and rub mixture deeply into flesh to produce rich golden color. Place in shallow pan with skin side up. Combine honey, orange rind, juice, salt, and pepper. Pour over chicken. Cover with foil and bake at 325° for 2 hours, basting frequently. Garnish with orange slices.

Nutritional Data

PER SERVING				EXCHANGES			
Calories:	309	Cholesterol (mg):	131	Milk:	0.0	Bread:	0.0
Fat (gm):	3	Sodium (mg):	148	Veg.:	0.0	Meat:	5.8
Sat. fat (gm):	.8	% Calories from fat:	9	Fruit:	1.0	Fat:	0.0

Salmon Dijonnaise

Yield: 4 servings

16 ounces salmon steaks
¼ cup yogurt
2 teaspoons prepared Dijon mustard
½ teaspoon **Hearty Mustard Blend**
1 Tablespoon soft diet margarine
¼ cup apple cider

Spread salmon steaks with paste made from yogurt, prepared Dijon, and Hearty Mustard Blend. Melt margarine in skillet; add cider. Saute salmon in cider-margarine mixture for 10 minutes on each side.

Nutritional Data

PER SERVING				EXCHANGES			
Calories:	192	Cholesterol (mg):	63.4	Milk:	0.1	Bread:	0.0
Fat (gm):	9	Sodium (mg):	106	Veg.:	0.0	Meat:	4.0
Sat. fat (gm):	1.5	% Calories from fat:	43	Fruit:	0.1	Fat:	0.3

GALLIC HERBES BLEND

3 Tablespoons dried chives
2 Tablespoons tarragon
1 Tablespoon chervil
1 Tablespoon parsley flakes

Skinny Spices Tip

Instead of spaghetti for the recipe above, try this low-calorie alternative: drain a large can of bean sprouts. Place the sprouts in fresh water and cook ½ hour until soft. Drain thoroughly. Pour sauce over sprouts. Trust me, it tastes a lot better than it sounds.

PARISIAN BISTRO STEAK

Yield: 6 servings

1½ pounds flank steak
¾ cup dry red wine
10 green onions, chopped
½ clove garlic, minced
1 teaspoon substitute salt
1 teaspoon rosemary
1 teaspoon pepper
¼ teaspoon **Gallic Herbes Blend**

Combine all ingredients and pour over flank steak. Marinate
1–2 hours, turning meat several times. Drain, reserving marinade. Broil
steak 3–4 minutes on each side, basting with marinade, until medium
rare. Cut diagonally, across grain of meat, into thin slices.

Nutritional Data

PER SERVING				EXCHANGES			
Calories:	260	Cholesterol (mg):	76.3	Milk:	0.0	Bread:	0.0
Fat (gm):	11.5	Sodium (mg):	98.4	Veg.:	0.1	Meat:	4.3
Sat. fat (gm):	5	% Calories from fat:	41	Fruit:	0.0	Fat:	0.4

ROSEMARY-SCENTED SPAGHETTI SAUCE

Yield: 1 serving

6 ounces no-salt-added tomato juice
½ Tablespoon sweet red onion
¼ teaspoon garlic powder
¼ teaspoon **Gallic Herbes Blend**
½ teaspoon rosemary
  Salt substitute to taste
  Pepper to taste
  Sugar substitute to taste
1 Tablespoon green peppers, finely chopped
1 Tablespoon mushrooms, finely chopped
1 teaspoon cornstarch

Simmer all ingredients together except mushrooms, green peppers, and cornstarch for 5 minutes. Add mushrooms and green peppers and simmer another 15 to 20 minutes. Dissolve cornstarch in a small amount of cold water and add to mixture. Cook until thickened and serve with pasta.

Nutritional Data

PER SERVING				EXCHANGES			
Calories:	58	Cholesterol (mg):	0	Milk:	0.0	Bread:	0.2
Fat (gm):	.3	Sodium (mg):	19.4	Veg.:	2.1	Meat:	0.0
Sat. fat (gm):	.1	% Calories from fat:	4	Fruit:	0.0	Fat:	0.0

11.

ITALIAN SPICE BLENDS

◆

California Chef's Pizza Blend
Presto Pesto Blend
Mamma Mia Pizza Blend
Checkered Tablecloth Italian Blend

◆

CALIFORNIA CHEF'S PIZZA BLEND

1 Tablespoon onion flakes
1 Tablespoon toasted sesame seeds
1 Tablespoon rosemary
1 Tablespoon basil
1 Tablespoon garlic
½ Tablespoon marjoram
½ Tablespoon oregano
½ Tablespoon ginger
½ Tablespoon mustard

Skinny Spices Tip

Spices that work well in recipes that include low-calorie, low-fat cheeses
include basil, caraway, celery seed, chervil, chili pepper, chives,
coriander, cumin, curry, dill, garlic, horseradish, lemon peel, marjoram,
mint, mustard, nutmeg, paprika, parsley, pepper, sage, tarragon,
and thyme.

SAN FRANCISCO ARTICHOKE HEARTS

Yield: 3 dozen

3 Tablespoons minced fresh onion
2 small cloves garlic, crushed
2 cups low-sodium chicken bouillon
3 10-ounce packages frozen artichoke hearts
4 Tablespoons lemon juice
1 teaspoon salt substitute
1½ teaspoons **California Chef's Pizza Blend**

Cook onion and garlic in bouillon until tender. Add artichoke hearts, lemon juice, salt substitute, and California Chef's Pizza Blend. Simmer for 5 minutes until tender. Drain, chill, and serve.

Nutritional Data

PER ARTICHOKE HEART

				EXCHANGES			
Calories:	12	Cholesterol (mg):	0	Milk:	0.0	Bread:	0.0
Fat (gm):	.1	Sodium (mg):	12.6	Veg.:	0.4	Meat:	0.0
Sat. fat (gm):	0	% Calories from fat:	8	Fruit:	0.0	Fat:	0.0

NOUVELLE PASTA SAUCE

Yield: 1 serving

4 ounces low-sodium tomato juice
1 packet low-sodium beef bouillon
1 Tablespoon dehydrated onion flakes
1 teaspoon **California Chef's Pizza Blend**
1 teaspoon parsley flakes
⅛ teaspoon garlic powder
    Salt substitute to taste
    Pepper to taste

Simmer all ingredients together for approximately 1 hour. Serve over pasta or spaghetti squash.

Nutritional Data

PER SERVING

				EXCHANGES			
Calories:	74	Cholesterol (mg):	1.8	Milk:	0.0	Bread:	0.3
Fat (gm):	1.7	Sodium (mg):	400	Veg.:	1.4	Meat:	0.3
Sat. fat (gm):	.8	% Calories from fat:	19	Fruit:	0.0	Fat:	0.1

PRESTO PESTO BLEND

4 Tablespoons basil
2 Tablespoons dried minced garlic
1 Tablespoon parsley flakes

Skinny Spices Tip

Instead of using oil to help crush fresh basil for pesto sauce, try low-sodium chicken bouillon or low-fat ricotta cheese.

PRESTO PESTO PASTA

Yield: 1 serving

2 ounces cooked pasta (any type)
1 Tablespoon olive oil
2 teaspoons **Presto Pesto Blend**
  Dash salt substitute to taste
  Dash pepper to taste
⅛ teaspoon Parmesan cheese

Toss cooked pasta with olive oil. Add Presto Pesto Blend, salt, and pepper. Garnish with Parmesan cheese.

Nutritional Data

PER SERVING				EXCHANGES			
Calories:	194	Cholesterol (mg):	.2	Milk: 0.0	Bread: 0.9
Fat (gm):	13.9	Sodium (mg):	12.8	Veg.: 0.0	Meat: 0.0
Sat. fat (gm):	1.9	% Calories from fat:	64	Fruit: 0.0	Fat: 2.6

UPTOWN BOW-TIES

Yield: 3 servings

1 Tablespoon canola oil
1 large clove garlic, minced
½ cup finely chopped onion
½ cup finely minced red bell pepper
½ cup minced yellow or green bell pepper
½ cup low-sodium chicken bouillon
2 Tablespoons **Presto Pesto Blend**
1 teaspoon red pepper flakes (optional)
7 ounces bow-tie pasta, cooked and drained

In a large non-stick skillet, heat oil over moderately high heat. Add garlic, onion, and bell peppers; saute for 4 minutes. Stir in broth, Presto Pesto Blend and red pepper flakes if desired. Bring to a boil, stirring occasionally. Reduce heat and simmer for 4 minutes. Spoon over pasta and toss. Can be chilled and served over salad greens.

Nutritional Data

PER SERVING				EXCHANGES			
Calories:	147	Cholesterol (mg):	0	Milk: 0.0	Bread: 1.1
Fat (gm):	5.1	Sodium (mg):	10.9	Veg.: 0.7	Meat: 0.0
Sat. fat (gm):	.4	% Calories from fat:	31	Fruit: 0.0	Fat: 0.9

MAMA MIA PIZZA BLEND

2 Tablespoons oregano
1 Tablespoon basil
½ Tablespoon onion flakes
½ Tablespoon garlic powder
½ Tablespoon thyme
½ Tablespoon fennel
½ Tablespoon paprika
½ Tablespoon coarsely ground
   black pepper
½ Tablespoon ginger
½ Tablespoon dried lemon peel

Skinny Spices Tip

Use fennel with oily fish to minimize the fishy taste. Also try fennel in stir-fry oriental combinations or sprinkle on top of pork.

PIZZA CRAVER'S PIZZA

Yield: 1 serving

⅓ cup no-salt-added tomato juice
⅛–¼ teaspoon dehydrated onion flakes (to taste)
Salt substitute to taste
⅛–¼ teaspoon **Mama Mia Pizza Blend** (to taste)
⅛–¼ teaspoon garlic powder (to taste)
1 teaspoon lemon juice
4 ounces canned salmon
1 slice low-calorie white bread
3 Tablespoons canned or fresh mushrooms

Simmer tomato juice with all seasonings and lemon juice. Break bread in very small pieces and put into bowl with salmon. Pour simmered mixture over bread and salmon and mix thoroughly. Press into 6-inch baking dish sprayed with non-stick vegetable spray. Arrange mushrooms on top. Bake in 350° oven for 15 minutes.

Nutritional Data

PER SERVING				EXCHANGES			
Calories:	235	Cholesterol (mg):	43.9	Milk:	0.0	Bread:	0.7
Fat (gm):	7.3	Sodium (mg):	659	Veg.:	0.8	Meat:	2.9
Sat. fat (gm):	1.8	% Calories from fat:	27	Fruit:	0.0	Fat:	0.0

ROMANTIC CLAM CHOWDER

Yield: 6 servings

2 cups no-salt-added tomato juice
Salt substitute to taste
1 12-ounce can clams with juice
1 teaspoon **Mama Mia Pizza Blend**
1–2 cloves garlic, finely chopped (to taste)
2 teaspoons "white" Worcestershire sauce

Simmer all ingredients together in pan or wok for 15 minutes. Serve hot with a garnish of fresh parsley or a twist of lemon rind.

Nutritional Data

PER SERVING				EXCHANGES			
Calories:	62	Cholesterol (mg):	20.1	Milk:	0.0	Bread:	0.0
Fat (gm):	.6	Sodium (mg):	118	Veg.:	0.7	Meat:	0.9
Sat. fat (gm):	.1	% Calories from fat:	9	Fruit:	0.0	Fat:	0.0

CHECKERED TABLECLOTH ITALIAN BLEND

1 Tablespoon garlic powder
1½ Tablespoons basil
1 Tablespoon thyme
1 Tablespoon oregano
1 Tablespoon rosemary
½ Tablespoon marjoram
½ Tablespoon sage
½ teaspoon cayenne pepper

Skinny Spices Tip

For a fresh Italian tomato salad, combine 3 plum tomatoes cut into rings, 5 fresh scallions (tops included), **Checkered Tablecloth Italian Blend** to taste, and a dash of salt substitute and pepper.

ITALIAN SEAFOOD SALAD

Yield: 6 servings

- ½ cup cooked crabmeat
- 1 cup cooked lobster meat
- ½ pound cooked shrimp
- 1 cup cooked white fish, flaked
- 2 tomatoes
- 1 cucumber, finely chopped
- 6 ripe olives, sliced
- ¼ cup plain low-fat yogurt
- ½ teaspoon celery seed
- ½ teaspoon salt substitute
- ½ teaspoon **Checkered Tablecloth Italian Blend**

Combine seafood with tomatoes, cucumber, and olives. Combine remaining ingredients for dressing and toss together. Serve in lettuce cups and garnish with pimento or parsley.

Nutritional Data

PER SERVING				EXCHANGES			
Calories:	151	Cholesterol (mg):	117	Milk:	0.1	Bread:	0.0
Fat (gm):	2.7	Sodium (mg):	271	Veg.:	0.6	Meat:	2.3
Sat. fat (gm):	.5	% Calories from fat:	17	Fruit:	0.0	Fat:	0.1

RAT-A-TATOUILLE

Yield: 6 servings

- 1 medium eggplant, peeled and diced
- 1 Tablespoon hot olive oil (available in gourmet stores and by mail)
- 2 large onions, chopped
- 2 green peppers, diced
- 2 cloves garlic, crushed
- 2 zucchini, diced
- 1 16-ounce can tomatoes
  Salt substitute to taste
  Pepper to taste
- 2 Tablespoons chopped parsley
- ¼ teaspoon **Checkered Tablecloth Italian Blend**

Saute eggplant in olive oil; add and saute onions, peppers, and garlic. When vegetables begin to soften, add zucchini and tomatoes. Add all remaining ingredients, including Checkered Tablecloth Italian Blend. Cover and simmer 25 minutes; remove cover and simmer 10 minutes more to reduce liquid.

Nutritional Data

PER SERVING				EXCHANGES			
Calories:	63	Cholesterol (mg):	0	Milk:	0.0	Bread:	0.0
Fat (gm):	2.6	Sodium (mg):	127	Veg.:	1.6	Meat:	0.0
Sat. fat (gm):	.4	% Calories from fat:	34	Fruit:	0.0	Fat:	0.4

12.
MEXICAN AND LATIN AMERICAN SPICE BLENDS

♦

Hot Cha Chili Blend
Mild Chili Magic Blend

♦

Hot Cha Chili Blend

1½ Tablespoons cumin
1 Tablespoon onion powder
1 Tablespoon garlic powder
½ Tablespoon ground ginger
½ Tablespoon paprika
½ Tablespoon oregano
½ Tablespoon dry mustard
½ Tablespoon cayenne pepper
½ Tablespoon parsley flakes

Skinny Spices Tip

This make-your-own molé mixture adds a fast dash of Mexican flavor to diet foods:

1 Tablespoon ground cumin
1 Tablespoon dried oregano
1 Tablespoon ground cinnamon
1 Tablespoon plain, unsweetened cocoa powder
4 Tablespoons chili powder

SOUTH-OF-THE-BORDER FRANKS

Yield: 8 servings

1 large onion
2 cloves garlic, minced
1 cup lite ketchup
2 teaspoons **Hot Cha Chili Blend**
1 Tablespoon dry mustard
1 Tablespoon salt substitute
1 pound turkey frankfurters

Put all ingredients, except franks, into large, heavy saucepan or kettle with 2 cups water. Bring to a boil, cover, and simmer 15 minutes. Add franks and simmer 10 minutes longer. Serve franks topped with half of sauce. Serve remaining sauce tableside.

Nutritional Data

PER SERVING				EXCHANGES			
Calories:	168	Cholesterol (mg):	49.1	Milk: 0.0	Bread: 0.0
Fat (gm):	10.2	Sodium (mg):	936	Veg.: 0.5	Meat: 1.3
Sat. fat (gm):	3.4	% Calories from fat:	53	Fruit: 0.5	Fat: 1.3

FLAME KISSED ROAST BEEF

Yield: 9 servings

3½ pounds sirloin of beef
2 teaspoons salt substitute
¾ teaspoon pepper
1 teaspoon **Hot Cha Chili Blend**
2 cloves garlic, minced
½ cup wine vinegar
½ cup water

Season meat with salt, pepper, Hot Cha Chili Blend and garlic. Marinate meat in fridge overnight in mixture of vinegar and water. Drain meat. Place meat on rack in roasting pan. Roast uncovered in a moderate oven at 350° until tender, allowing 20–22 minutes per pound for medium-well done.

Nutritional Data

PER SERVING				EXCHANGES			
Calories:	501	Cholesterol (mg):	159	Milk: 0.0	Bread: 0.0
Fat (gm):	32.6	Sodium (mg):	110	Veg.: 0.0	Meat: 6.2
Sat. fat (gm):	13.5	% Calories from fat:	60	Fruit: 0.0	Fat: 3.1

Mild Chili Magic Blend

2 Tablespoons chili powder
1 Tablespoon cumin
1 Tablespoon oregano
1 Tablespoon garlic
1 Tablespoon salt substitute

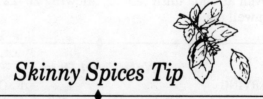

Skinny Spices Tip

Cumin seeds add South-of-the-Border flair to salads. Use about ⅛ teaspoon, along with a teaspoon of crumbled oregano. Serve with a cool, diet ranch dressing.

MEXICALI ROSE CHIP DIP

Yield: 16 servings

1 cup plain low-fat yogurt
2 teaspoons grated orange rind
¼ teaspoon **Mild Chili Magic Blend**
1 small dash granulated sugar substitute

Combine ingredients, refrigerate and use as a dip for carrot chips, fresh mushrooms, green pepper, and cauliflower florets.

Nutritional Data

PER SERVING				EXCHANGES			
Calories:	10	Cholesterol (mg):	.9	Milk:	0.1	Bread:	0.0
Fat (gm):	.2	Sodium (mg):	10.8	Veg.:	0.0	Meat:	0.0
Sat. fat (gm):	.2	% Calories from fat:	22	Fruit:	0.0	Fat:	0.0

FIESTA BURGERS

Yield: 8 burgers

2 pounds ground chuck
1 Tablespoon dehydrated minced onion
1½ teaspoons salt substitute
¾ teaspoon **Mild Chili Magic Blend**
¼ teaspoon pepper
⅛ teaspoon garlic powder

Combine all ingredients and mix lightly. Shape into 8 patties, each about ½-inch thick, and pan broil in hot skillet until desired doneness (bake if desired).

Nutritional Data

PER BURGER				EXCHANGES			
Calories:	285	Cholesterol (mg):	120	Milk:	0.0	Bread:	0.0
Fat (gm):	14.9	Sodium (mg):	80.6	Veg.:	0.1	Meat:	5.1
Sat. fat (gm):	5.8	% Calories from fat:	48	Fruit:	0.0	Fat:	0.0

COWBOY CHILI

Yield: 3 servings

3 Tablespoons soft diet margarine
1 green pepper
2 ounces onions, cut thin
6 ounces extra-lean ground beef
8 ounces low-sodium tomato juice
1 Tablespoon **Mild Chili Magic Blend**
  Salt substitute to taste
  Pepper to taste
8 ounces bean sprouts, drained (optional)

Saute green pepper and onion in margarine, using non-stick pan that has also been coated with non-stick spray. Add crumbled ground beef and cook for 10 minutes, stirring constantly. Drain fat before adding tomato juice, Mild Chili Magic Blend, salt, and pepper. Cook until done. Add bean sprouts if extra volume is desired.

Nutritional Data

PER SERVING				EXCHANGES			
Calories:	235	Cholesterol (mg):	56.1	Milk:	0.0	Bread:	0.0
Fat (gm):	14.7	Sodium (mg):	211	Veg.:	1.4	Meat:	2.0
Sat. fat (gm):	4.5	% Calories from fat:	55	Fruit:	0.0	Fat:	1.8

13.
CHINESE
SPICE
BLEND

♦
Hunan Blend
♦

HUNAN BLEND

2 Tablespoons toasted sesame seeds
1 Tablespoon ground black pepper
1 Tablespoon garlic
1 Tablespoon ground ginger
1 Tablespoon dried cilantro
½ Tablespoon mustard seed
½ teaspoon cayenne pepper

Skinny Spices Tip

Here's a quick, tasty side dish that's a cool complement to spicy Chinese food: marinate cucumber slices and onion rings in rice vinegar. Add a dash of liquid sugar substitute. Sprinkle with toasted sesame seeds and serve.

Plum Delicious Chinese Chicken

Yield: 4 servings

2 lbs. chicken breasts, split, with skin
6 ripe purple plums, pitted and thinly sliced
1 onion, halved and thinly sliced
1 clove garlic, minced
3 Tablespoons water
2 Tablespoons lemon juice
2 Tablespoons light soy sauce
½ teaspoon liquid sugar substitute
1 teaspoon **Hunan Blend**

Brown chicken, skin side down, in an ungreased non-stick skillet or chicken fryer. Drain and discard chicken fat. Blot chicken with paper towel, remove skin, and return to the pan, skin side up. Add remaining ingredients *except low-calorie sweetener*. Cover and simmer, stirring occasionally, until chicken is tender, 40–45 minutes. Uncover and continue simmering until sauce is thick. Add low-calorie sweetener only after cooking is complete and skillet has been removed from heat.

Nutritional Data

PER SERVING				EXCHANGES			
Calories:	419	Cholesterol (mg):	145	Milk:	0.0	Bread:	0.0
Fat (gm):	21.2	Sodium (mg):	144	Veg.:	0.3	Meat:	6.3
Sat. fat (gm):	6.1	% Calories from fat:	47	Fruit:	0.3	Fat:	0.0

SPICY SZECHUAN ALL-VEGETABLE STIR-FRY

Yield: 4 servings

1 Tablespoon plus 1 teaspoon peanut oil
3 cups diagonally sliced asparagus (trim woody
ends from 1 lb. asparagus)
1 cup diagonally sliced carrots
1 cup diagonally sliced celery
1 cup thinly sliced onions
1 medium red bell pepper, cut into strips
1 garlic clove, finely minced
¾ cup hot water
2 teaspoons dry sherry
2 teaspoons oyster sauce
1 teaspoon **Hunan Blend**
1 packet low-sodium beef bouillon
1 teaspoon cornstarch

Heat large wok or skillet; add oil and tilt wok or skillet to coat it
evenly. Add vegetables, one at a time in order listed, stir-frying each for
1 minute. Add garlic and stir-fry for about 1 minute longer. In
measuring cup or bowl, combine remaining ingredients, stirring to
dissolve cornstarch; pour over vegetables, and cook until thick. Cover
wok or skillet, reduce heat, and let cook until vegetables are tender-crisp
or done to taste.

Nutritional Data

PER SERVING				EXCHANGES			
Calories:	128	Cholesterol (mg):	0	Milk:	0.0	Bread:	0.0
Fat (gm):	4.9	Sodium (mg):	200	Veg.:	0.0	Meat:	0.0
Sat. fat (gm):	.8	% Calories from fat:	31	Fruit:	0.0	Fat:	0.0

14.
JAPANESE SPICE BLENDS

♦

Garlic & Ginger Blend
Japanese Horseradish Blend

♦

GARLIC & GINGER BLEND

3 Tablespoons ground ginger
1½ Tablespoons garlic powder or granules
1 Tablespoon dried lemon peel
1 Tablespoon mustard powder
½ Tablespoon dashi (dried fish stock
found in Japanese or oriental import
stores or available by mail)

Skinny Spices Tip

Ground ginger makes diet oil-and-vinegar salad dressings sparkle. Use
⅛ teaspoon per cup of dressing.

BEEF STRIPS HAWAIIAN

Yield: 4 servings

- 1 lb. round steak, cut 2 inches thick
- 1½ teaspoons dry mustard
- ¾ teaspoon **Garlic & Ginger Blend**
- 1½ teaspoons black pepper
- ½ clove minced garlic to taste
- 6 Tablespoons low-sodium soy sauce
- 3 Tablespoons lemon juice
- 1 small eggplant, cubed
- 8 whole mushrooms

Chill steak well or partially freeze to make cutting into 1-inch strips easier. Place these strips in a shallow pan. Combine mustard, Garlic & Ginger Blend, pepper, and garlic with soy sauce and lemon juice. Pour over steak strips and marinate at least 4 hours. Parboil eggplant cubes 5 minutes, then drain. Thread steak strips on metal skewers, alternating with vegetables. Brush with marinade and broil 4 inches from heat, 6–7 minutes on each side.

Nutritional Data

PER SERVING				EXCHANGES			
Calories:	296	Cholesterol (mg):	81.7	Milk:	0.0	Bread:	0.0
Fat (gm):	16.3	Sodium (mg):	770	Veg.:	0.8	Meat:	4.0
Sat. fat (gm):	6.3	% Calories from fat:	50	Fruit:	0.0	Fat:	0.0

14 CARROTS GOLD

Yield: 4 servings

- 2 cups sliced carrots
- Water, salted with salt substitute
- 2 Tablespoons soft diet margarine
- ½ teaspoon **Garlic & Ginger Blend**
- Grated rind of ½ orange

Cook carrots in boiling, salted water 5–8 minutes and drain well. Melt diet margarine, and mix in Garlic & Ginger Blend and grated orange rind. Coat carrots thoroughly.

Nutritional Data

PER SERVING				EXCHANGES			
Calories:	73	Cholesterol (mg):	0	Milk:	0.0	Bread:	0.0
Fat (gm):	3	Sodium (mg):	64.7	Veg.:	1.6	Meat:	0.0
Sat. fat (gm):	.5	% Calories from fat:	35	Fruit:	0.0	Fat:	0.5

JAPANESE HORSERADISH BLEND

5 Tablespoons wasabi (Japanese horseradish powder found in Japanese or oriental import stores or available by mail)
2 Tablespoons garlic powder

Skinny Spices Tip

Japanese horseradish (*wasabi*) also comes in paste form. Try blending a small amount (it's hot stuff!) with low-fat cottage cheese or ricotta cheese for a lively dip.

DRESSING WITH A KICK

Yield: 16 servings

1 cup plain low-fat yogurt
¼ teaspoon **Japanese Horseradish Blend**
1 Tablespoon tarragon vinegar
1 Tablespoon chopped dill
1 Tablespoon chopped chives
1 Tablespoon sugar
¾ teaspoon salt substitute
¼ teaspoon paprika

Combine all ingredients. Cover and chill at least 4 hours.

Nutritional Data

PER SERVING				EXCHANGES			
Calories:	7	Cholesterol (mg):	.5	Milk:	0.1	Bread:	0.0
Fat (gm):	.1	Sodium (mg):	5.4	Veg.:	0.0	Meat:	0.0
Sat. fat (gm):	.1	% Calories from fat:	17	Fruit:	0.0	Fat:	0.0

WASABI BUTTER SOLE

Yield: 2 servings

2 Tablespoons all-purpose flour
¼ teaspoon salt substitute
  Dash pepper
  Dash onion powder
  Dash garlic powder
  Dash paprika
2 sole fillets, 5 ounces each
1 Tablespoon plus 1 teaspoon soft diet
  margarine
½ teaspoon **Japanese Horseradish Blend**
1 Tablespoon chopped parsley

On sheet of wax paper, thoroughly combine flour and seasonings
except for Japanese Horseradish Blend. Dredge fillets in mixture,
coating evenly. In medium-size skillet, heat margarine until bubbly and
hot; stir in Japanese Horseradish Blend. Add fish and cook over medium
heat until browned on both sides. Sprinkle with parsley.

Nutritional Data

PER SERVING				EXCHANGES			
Calories:	209	Cholesterol (mg):	78.2	Milk:	0.0	Bread:	0.4
Fat (gm):	5.6	Sodium (mg):	166	Veg.:	0.0	Meat:	5.7
Sat. fat (gm):	1.1	% Calories from fat:	25	Fruit:	0.0	Fat:	0.7

15.

INDIAN
SPICE
BLENDS

◆

Ceylon Curry Blend
Whisper of India Mild Curry Blend
Custom Curry Medium-Hot Blend

◆

CEYLON CURRY BLEND

3 Tablespoons curry powder
2 Tablespoons cardamon
1 Tablespoon cinnamon
1 Tablespoon ground black or
  cayenne pepper

Skinny Spices Tip

For deliciously different deviled eggs, mash the yolks of hard boiled eggs
with vinegar or lemon juice, powdered mustard, garlic, black pepper, a
dash of curry powder, and low-calorie mayonnaise.

SIMPLY DIVINE CURRY

Yield: 16 servings

- 2 chickens (4 pounds), cut in pieces, skin removed
- 1 cup plain low-fat yogurt
- 1 medium onion, finely chopped
- 2 cups water
- 1 green pepper, diced
- ½–1 Tablespoon **Ceylon Curry Blend** (to taste)
- ½ teaspoon salt substitute

Brown chicken pieces on all sides under broiler. Remove to a large pot or wok. Cover chicken with onions, yogurt, water, and Ceylon Curry Blend and simmer 15 minutes. Add green pepper and salt, and simmer 20–30 minutes or more until chicken is tender.

Nutritional Data

PER SERVING				EXCHANGES			
Calories:	210	Cholesterol (mg):	73.5	Milk:	0.1	Bread:	0.0
Fat (gm):	10.7	Sodium (mg):	82.6	Veg.:	0.2	Meat:	3.1
Sat. fat (gm):	3.2	% Calories from fat:	47	Fruit:	0.0	Fat:	0.0

SPECIAL "SOUR CREAM" PARTY DIP

Yield: 16 servings

- ⅔ cup low-fat cottage cheese
- 1 Tablespoon skim milk
- 1 Tablespoon lemon juice
- ¼–½ teaspoon **Ceylon Curry Blend** to taste

Dry-roast Ceylon Curry Blend in pan or toaster oven 1-2 minutes until fragrant; do not burn ingredients. Blend all ingredients in electric blender, adding slightly more milk and lemon juice if necessary.

Nutritional Data

PER SERVING				EXCHANGES			
Calories:	8	Cholesterol (mg):	.5	Milk:	0.0	Bread:	0.0
Fat (gm):	.1	Sodium (mg):	43.5	Veg.:	0.0	Meat:	0.2
Sat. fat (gm):	.1	% Calories from fat:	12	Fruit:	0.0	Fat:	0.0

WHISPER OF INDIA MILD CURRY BLEND

1 Tablespoon ground ginger
1 Tablespoon garlic powder
1 Tablespoon turmeric
½ Tablespoon ground coriander
½ Tablespoon cumin
½ Tablespoon black pepper
½ Tablespoon mustard
½ Tablespoon fennel
½ Tablespoon cayenne pepper
½ Tablespoon allspice

Skinny Spices Tip

For a quick, homemade curry powder, try this variation:

1½ Tablespoons ground coriander
1½ Tablespoons cumin
1 Tablespoon ground ginger
½ Tablespoon black pepper
½ Tablespoon red cayenne pepper

Nirvana Veggies

Yield: 10 servings

1 head cauliflower, broken into florets
1 16-ounce bag frozen whole baby carrots
1 cup chopped green pepper
1 cup water
1 teaspoon salt substitute
3 Tablespoons canola oil
¼ teaspoon **Whisper of India Mild Curry Blend**

Combine all ingredients except oil and Whisper of India Mild Curry Blend; bring to a boil. Simmer, covered, until all vegetables are tender, about 15 minutes. Drain, coat with oil and Whisper of India Mild Curry Blend, and saute 3 minutes to combine flavors.

Nutritional Data

PER SERVING				EXCHANGES			
Calories:	59	Cholesterol (mg):	0	Milk:	0.0	Bread:	0.0
Fat (gm):	4.2	Sodium (mg):	16.6	Veg.:	0.7	Meat:	0.0
Sat. fat (gm):	.3	% Calories from fat:	61	Fruit:	0.0	Fat:	0.8

Mughal Potato Curry

Yield: 6 servings

1 Tablespoon soft diet margarine
1 onion halved and sliced
1 green bell pepper, seeded and diced
3 potatoes, peeled and quartered
1 cup low-sodium chicken bouillon (or use 1 cup chicken broth skimmed of fat)
1½ teaspoons **Whisper of India Mild Curry Blend**
3 Tablespoons minced fresh parsley

In a saucepan, melt the margarine over moderate heat. Add onion and cook, stirring until translucent. Stir in pepper and potatoes. Add bouillon (or broth) and Whisper of India Mild Curry Blend. Cover and simmer until potatoes are nearly tender; about 20 minutes. Uncover and simmer until most of the liquid evaporates. Add minced parsley just before serving.

Nutritional Data

PER SERVING			EXCHANGES			
Calories:	92	Cholesterol (mg):	0	Milk: 0.0	Bread: 1.0
Fat (gm):	1.1	Sodium (mg):	150	Veg.: 0.4	Meat: 0.0
Sat. fat (gm):	.2	% Calories from fat:	10	Fruit: 0.0	Fat: 0.2

CUSTOM CURRY MEDIUM-HOT BLEND

1 Tablespoon mustard powder
1 Tablespoon ground ginger
1 Tablespoon turmeric
1 Tablespoon cumin
1 Tablespoon allspice
1 Tablespoon cayenne pepper
½ Tablespoon fennel

Skinny Spices Tip

For a homemade version of Garam masala, an Indian spice blend
required in many authentic recipes, use whole spices and grind the
following ingredients into a powder:

2 Tablespoons black peppercorns
1½ Tablespoons cumin seeds
2 Tablespoons coriander seeds
1 Tablespoon cardamon seeds
1 inch cinnamon stick
5 cloves

SCALLOPS TAJ MAHAL

Yield: 20 skewers

1 pound bay scallops (or sea scallops cut in half)
2 cups cherry tomatoes
2 large green peppers cut into 1-inch pieces
⅓ cup lemon juice
2 Tablespoons unsweetened pineapple juice mixed with 1 packet of sugar substitute to sweeten
2 Tablespoons prepared mustard
1 Tablespoon canola oil
1½ teaspoons **Custom Curry Medium-Hot Blend**

Alternate scallops, tomatoes, and green peppers on 20 metal or wooden skewers. Place kabobs on well-oiled broiler pan. Combine remaining ingredients, and brush kabobs with this medium-hot sauce. Broil 4 inches from heat source for 3–5 minutes. Turn, brush with sauce, broil 3–5 minutes more, basting once.

Nutritional Data

PER SKEWER				EXCHANGES			
Calories:	40	Cholesterol (mg):	7.2	Milk: 0.0		Bread: 0.0
Fat (gm):	1.6	Sodium (mg):	63.8	Veg.: 0.3		Meat: 0.4
Sat. fat (gm):	.2	% Calories from fat:	34	Fruit: 0.0		Fat: 0.1

MADRAS SALMON

Yield: 1 serving

4 ounces canned salmon
1 Tablespoon non-fat dry milk in dry form
⅓ cup water
½ packet low-sodium chicken bouillon
¼ teaspoon **Custom Curry Medium-Hot Blend**
1 slice toast, using 40-calorie white bread

Mix salmon, milk, water, and Custom Curry Medium-Hot Blend in saucepan and heat. Add bouillon and stir in thoroughly. Pour over toast.

Nutritional Data

PER SERVING				EXCHANGES			
Calories:	234	Cholesterol (mg):	44.7	Milk: 0.2		Bread: 0.7
Fat (gm):	7.2	Sodium (mg):	699	Veg.: 0.0		Meat: 2.9
Sat. fat (gm):	1.9	% Calories from fat:	28	Fruit: 0.0		Fat: 0.0

16.
THAI SPICE BLENDS

♦

Coriander Blend
Bangkok Spice Blend

♦

CORIANDER BLEND

1½ Tablespoons red bell pepper flakes
1½ Tablespoons coriander seeds
1½ Tablespoons coarsely ground black
   pepper
1½ Tablespoons ground cloves
 1 Tablespoon ground ginger

Skinny Spices Tip

For another Thai spice blend variation, combine chili peppers, dried cilantro, cumin, garlic powder, and onion powder.

ZESTY CORNED BEEF

Yield: approx. 8 servings

2 pounds lean corned beef (not brisket)
  Water to cover
½ onion, sliced
2 cloves garlic, chopped
5 bay leaves
2 Tablespoons **Coriander Blend**

Place corned beef in a pot with water, cover, and simmer for 30 minutes. Discard water and replace with fresh water. Add onion, garlic, bay leaves, and Coriander Blend. Cover and simmer until meat is fork-tender, 45–60 minutes, depending on size. Let cool to room temperature, then discard water and spices. Chill and slice thin.

Nutritional Data

PER SERVING				EXCHANGES			
Calories:	286	Cholesterol (mg):	111	Milk:	0.0	Bread:	0.0
Fat (gm):	21.4	Sodium (mg):	1283	Veg.:	0.1	Meat:	0.3
Sat. fat (gm):	7.2	% Calories from fat:	69	Fruit:	0.0	Fat:	2.7

GOLDEN TEMPLE CHICKEN

Yield: 4 servings

4 pieces frying chicken thighs (or equivalent
  chicken parts), skinless
4 Tablespoons plain low-fat yogurt
2 Tablespoons lemon juice
2 Tablespoons vinegar
3 teaspoons **Coriander Blend**

Combine all ingredients (except chicken) for marinade. Cover chicken with mixture and refrigerate several hours. Arrange thighs in shallow broiler tray. Broil 6 inches from heat source for 15 minutes, turning and basting frequently with pan juices. Move 3 inches closer to heat source and broil. Turn frequently for 10–15 minutes longer until juices run clear.

Nutritional Data

PER SERVING				EXCHANGES			
Calories:	211	Cholesterol (mg):	79.9	Milk:	0.1	Bread:	0.0
Fat (gm):	14.5	Sodium (mg):	82.3	Veg.:	0.0	Meat:	2.3
Sat. fat (gm):	4.2	% Calories from fat:	63	Fruit:	0.0	Fat:	1.5

Bangkok Spice Blend

2½ Tablespoons toasted sesame seeds
½ Tablespoon onion
½ Tablespoon chili powder
½ Tablespoon garlic
½ Tablespoon cayenne pepper
½ Tablespoon coriander
½ Tablespoon nutmeg
½ Tablespoon cinnamon
½ Tablespoon dried lemon peel

Skinny Spices Tip

Try this flavorful sweet-and-spicy blend that's great on chicken or fish:
cinnamon, ginger, pepper, and star anise.

Shrimp Curry Salad

Yield: 4 servings

- 2 cups cooked (1 lb. frozen) or 2 cans of shrimp sprinkled with lemon juice
- ½ cup diced apple
- ½ cup celery and leaves
- ¼ cup diced green pepper
- ½ teaspoon salt substitute
- ¼ teaspoon curry powder
- ¼ teaspoon **Bangkok Spice Blend**
- ¼ cup low-calorie mayonnaise
- Lettuce leaves

Combine shrimp with apples, celery, and green pepper. Add salt and spices to low-calorie mayonnaise. Combine with salad mixture and toss lightly. Arrange in chilled lettuce cups.

Nutritional Data

PER SERVING				EXCHANGES			
Calories:	148	Cholesterol (mg):	221	Milk: 0.0		Bread: 0.0	
Fat (gm):	1.4	Sodium (mg):	447	Veg.: 0.3		Meat: 2.0	
Sat. fat (gm):	.4	% Calories from fat:	9	Fruit: 0.5		Fat: 0.0	

Siam Stuffed Peppers

Yield: 2 servings

- 8 ounces water-packed tuna, well drained and flaked
- ½ cup celery, chopped
- 1 teaspoon dehydrated onion flakes, to taste
- 3 Tablespoons cider vinegar
- Salt substitute to taste
- Freshly ground black pepper
- ¼ teaspoon **Bangkok Spice Blend**
- 4 large green peppers

Blend tuna, chopped celery, dehydrated onion flakes, salt, pepper, Bangkok Spice Blend, and vinegar in a bowl. Chill for ½ hour. Remove tops from peppers and scoop out insides to make a cup. Sprinkle salt substitute on the insides of peppers. Spoon in tuna mixture and serve on bed of lettuce.

Nutritional Data

PER SERVING				EXCHANGES			
Calories:	181	Cholesterol (mg):	34.1	Milk:	0.0	Bread:	0.0
Fat (gm):	1.3	Sodium (mg):	413	Veg.:	1.7	Meat:	2.3
Sat. fat (gm):	.3	% Calories from fat:	6	Fruit:	0.0	Fat:	0.0

17.
RUSSIAN AND HUNGARIAN SPICE BLENDS

◆

Old Country Caraway Blend
Paprika Blend

◆

OLD COUNTRY CARAWAY BLEND

3 Tablespoons caraway
2 Tablespoons garlic powder
½ teaspoon black or cayenne pepper

Skinny Spices Tip

For hearty coleslaw without added fat, add ¼ teaspoon of anise seeds. This is an especially nice addition when the slaw contains bits of pineapple or chopped apple.

Vegetable Hater's Brussels Sprouts

Yield: 4 servings

8 ounces canned tomatoes
1 green pepper, chopped
1 bay leaf
1 teaspoon **Old Country Caraway Blend**
½ teaspoon paprika
Salt substitute to taste
Pepper to taste
8 ounces Brussels sprouts, cooked and drained

Combine all ingredients except Brussels sprouts and simmer 8–10 minutes, until green pepper is tender. Cut cooked sprouts in half and combine with tomato mixture. Heat thoroughly.

Nutritional Data

PER SERVING				EXCHANGES			
Calories:	41	Cholesterol (mg):	0	Milk:	0.0	Bread:	0.0
Fat (gm):	.3	Sodium (mg):	107	Veg.:	1.3	Meat:	0.0
Sat. fat (gm):	.1	% Calories from fat:	6	Fruit:	0.0	Fat:	0.0

Sweet 'n Sour Ambrosia

Yield: 4 servings

¼ cup low-fat plain yogurt
2 teaspoons white wine vinegar
½ teaspoon **Old Country Caraway Blend**
½ teaspoon salt substitute
½ teaspoon fresh lemon juice
2 cups thinly sliced celery
2 small Golden Delicious apples, cored and diced
¼ cup dark raisins
8 lettuce leaves

In medium bowl, combine yogurt, vinegar, Old Country Caraway Blend, salt, and lemon juice, mixing well. Add remaining ingredients except lettuce and blend thoroughly to combine. Chill for 30 minutes before serving.

Nutritional Data

PER SERVING				EXCHANGES			
Calories:	91	Cholesterol (mg):	.9	Milk:	0.1	Bread:	0.0
Fat (gm):	.6	Sodium (mg):	64.2	Veg.:	0.3	Meat:	0.0
Sat. fat (gm):	.2	% Calories from fat:	6	Fruit:	1.3	Fat:	0.0

Paprika Blend

3½ Tablespoons paprika
3½ Tablespoons dill

Skinny Spices Tip

There are two types of paprika: the more pungent Hungarian variety is
a must for goulash and chicken paprikash. The milder Spanish variety,
the most common type found in the United States, is used mainly as
a garnish.

Delectable Herb Dressing

Yield: 16 servings

- 2 teaspoons prepared horseradish
- 1 Tablespoon tarragon vinegar
- ¼ cup lemon juice
- ¾ cup water
  Sugar substitute to equal 1 Tablespoon of sugar
- 1 teaspoon salt substitute
- 1 teaspoon **Paprika Blend**
- 2 cups non-fat dry milk powder

Combine all ingredients in electric blender. Blend for 30 seconds or until smooth. Chill for about 2 hours.

Nutritional Data

PER SERVING				EXCHANGES			
Calories:	32	Cholesterol (mg):	1.6	Milk:	0.3	Bread:	0.0
Fat (gm):	.1	Sodium (mg):	47.3	Veg.:	0.0	Meat:	0.0
Sat. fat (gm):	0	% Calories from fat:	2	Fruit:	0.0	Fat:	0.0

Incredible Edible Spread

Yield: 1 serving

- 4 ounces water-packed tuna, drained
- 1 teaspoon dehydrated onion flakes
- 2 teaspoons **Paprika Blend**
- 2 teaspoons non-fat dry milk
- 1 Tablespoon water
  Celery and green pepper slices

Place all ingredients except celery and green pepper slices in electric blender or food processor. Blend or process at low speed for 30 seconds. Garnish with celery and green pepper slices.

Nutritional Data

PER SERVING				EXCHANGES			
Calories:	145	Cholesterol (mg):	34.6	Milk:	0.1	Bread:	0.0
Fat (gm):	1	Sodium (mg):	399	Veg.:	0.2	Meat:	2.3
Sat. fat (gm):	.3	% Calories from fat:	6	Fruit:	0.0	Fat:	0.0

18.
GREEK
AND
MID-EASTERN
SPICE BLENDS

◆

Garlic & Lemon Twist Blend
Open Sesame Blend
Moroccan Mint Blend
Savory Tarragon Blend

◆

GARLIC & LEMON TWIST BLEND

2 Tablespoons garlic powder
2 Tablespoons dried lemon peel
1 Tablespoon coarsely ground black pepper
1 Tablespoon finely ground green pepper
1 Tablespoon finely ground white or pink pepper

Skinny Spices Tip

For a quick summer herb blend, combine basil, marjoram, rosemary, and thyme.

VESTAL VIRGINS' DIP

Yield: 16 servings

1 clove fresh garlic, finely minced
3 walnut meats, grated
1 teaspoon olive oil
1 cup plain, low-fat yogurt
1 small, unpeeled cucumber, diced
¼ teaspoon **Garlic & Lemon Twist Blend**

Combine garlic and nuts with oil in food processor, and puree into a smooth paste. Stir into yogurt, add cucumber, season with Garlic & Lemon Twist Blend to taste. Refrigerate several hours to combine flavors. Great as a dip for cucumbers, carrots, zucchini, and green peppers.

Nutritional Data

PER SERVING				EXCHANGES			
Calories:	24	Cholesterol (mg):	.9	Milk: 0.1		Bread: 0.0
Fat (gm):	1.4	Sodium (mg):	11.3	Veg.: 0.1		Meat: 0.0
Sat. fat (gm):	.3	% Calories from fat:	51	Fruit: 0.0		Fat: 0.1

BELLY DANCER'S CAULIFLOWER

Yield: 4 servings

1 whole cauliflower
½ cup chicken bouillon from low-sodium granules
1 Tablespoon low-sodium soy sauce
1 teaspoon **Garlic & Lemon Twist Blend**

Simmer cauliflower in chicken bouillon until tender about 20 minutes. Drain and sprinkle with soy sauce and Garlic & Lemon Twist Blend.

Nutritional Data

PER SERVING				EXCHANGES			
Calories:	37	Cholesterol (mg):	0	Milk: 0.0		Bread: 0.0
Fat (gm):	.4	Sodium (mg):	200	Veg.: 1.0		Meat: 0.0
Sat. fat (gm):	.1	% Calories from fat:	6	Fruit: 0.0		Fat: 0.0

Open Sesame Blend

4 Tablespoons toasted sesame seeds
1 Tablespoon onion flakes
½ Tablespoon paprika
½ Tablespoon garlic powder
½ Tablespoon dried lemon peel
½ Tablespoon cayenne pepper

Skinny Spices Tip

Enhance the nutty flavor of sesame seeds by toasting or browning before adding them to salads for a nutritious topping. Toast by spreading seeds on a shallow cooking tin in a hot oven for a few minutes. Or shake them in a non-stick skillet over high heat. Let cool and store in covered jar.

CUTE AS CAN BE CUKES

◆

Yield: 4 servings

- 2 medium cucumbers
- 2 teaspoons salt substitute
- ½ cup white vinegar
- 1½ teaspoons liquid sugar substitute
- 2 teaspoons minced fresh ginger root
- 2 teaspoons **Open Sesame Blend**

Wash cucumbers and pare lengthwise into ¼-inch strips, leaving every other strip of green skin on. Cut in halves, lengthwise, remove seeds, and slice thinly. Put in bowl and add salt substitute. Mix well and let stand 1 hour. Place cucumbers in cheesecloth and squeeze out any excess moisture. Mix remaining ingredients and bring to a boil. Pour over cucumbers and chill several hours.

Nutritional Data

PER SERVING				EXCHANGES			
Calories:	33	Cholesterol (mg):	0	Milk:	0.0	Bread:	0.0
Fat (gm):	.9	Sodium (mg):	3.6	Veg.:	0.7	Meat:	0.0
Sat. fat (gm):	.2	% Calories from fat:	22	Fruit:	0.1	Fat:	0.2

CURRIED SESAME SAUCE

◆

Yield: 8 servings

- ½ cup buttermilk
- 1 Tablespoon bottled white horseradish
- 2 Tablespoons low-sodium ketchup
- 1 teaspoon lemon juice
- 1 teaspoon curry powder
- 2 teaspoons **Open Sesame Blend**
- ½ teaspoon finely ground pepper

Combine all ingredients, mix thoroughly, and chill.

Nutritional Data

PER SERVING				EXCHANGES			
Calories:	15	Cholesterol (mg):	.5	Milk:	0.1	Bread:	0.0
Fat (gm):	.5	Sodium (mg):	63.3	Veg.:	0.1	Meat:	0.0
Sat. fat (gm):	.1	% Calories from fat:	29	Fruit:	0.1	Fat:	0.1

MOROCCAN MINT BLEND

2 Tablespoons dried mint leaves
2 Tablespoons garlic granules or powder
2 Tablespoons toasted sesame seeds
½ Tablespoon dried lemon peel
½ Tablespoon onion flakes

Skinny Spices Tip

Do as the French do, and toss some melted diet margarine and mint into cooked vegetables just before serving.

LAMB KABOBS

Yield: 6 servings

- 1 teaspoon **Moroccan Mint Blend**
- ½ cup dry red wine
- ¼ cup red wine vinegar
- 1 clove garlic, minced
- 1 teaspoon salt substitute
- ¼ teaspoon pepper
- 1½ pounds boned lamb, cut into 1-inch cubes

Combine Moroccan Mint Blend, wine, vinegar, garlic, salt, and pepper. Pour over lamb and marinate at least 1 hour. Drain, reserving marinade. Place lamb on skewers and broil 20 minutes, coating frequently with marinade.

Nutritional Data

PER SERVING				EXCHANGES			
Calories:	234	Cholesterol (mg):	101	Milk:	0.0	Bread:	0.0
Fat (gm):	8.8	Sodium (mg):	78.4	Veg.:	0.0	Meat:	4.0
Sat. fat (gm):	3.1	% Calories from fat:	35	Fruit:	0.1	Fat:	0.3

MARAKESH DELIGHT CREAM SOUP

Yield: 4 cups

- 1 cup plain low-fat yogurt
- ¼ cup all-purpose flour
- 4 cups low-sodium chicken broth
- ½ teaspoon **Moroccan Mint Blend**

Stir yogurt and flour together in a saucepan. Gradually add chicken broth, bring to a boil, and stir over medium heat for 5 minutes. Add Moroccan Mint Blend and heat for 1 minute more. Serve hot or cold, and garnish with fresh parsley or a mint leaf.

Nutritional Data

PER CUP				EXCHANGES			
Calories:	67	Cholesterol (mg):	3.7	Milk:	0.4	Bread:	0.4
Fat (gm):	1	Sodium (mg):	43.2	Veg.:	0.0	Meat:	0.0
Sat. fat (gm):	.6	% Calories from fat:	14	Fruit:	0.0	Fat:	0.1

Savory Tarragon Blend

2 Tablespoons tarragon
1 Tablespoon onion flakes
1 Tablespoon mustard powder
1 Tablespoon black pepper
1 Tablespoon fennel
1 Tablespoon savory

Skinny Spices Tip

Savory is a great complement to bean dishes. It's also good with game, roast turkey, and low-calorie meat loaf.

GRECIAN GODDESS ZUCCHINI

Yield: 10 servings

1 Tablespoon chopped parsley
1 teaspoon **Savory Tarragon Blend**
  Pinch thyme
½ teaspoon salt substitute
  Dash pepper
2 drops hot sauce
1 bay leaf
2 Tablespoons lemon juice
2 cloves garlic, minced fine
1 cup red wine
1 pound zucchini, sliced ¼-inch thick

Combine all ingredients except zucchini in saucepan. Bring to a boil, then add zucchini and simmer 5–10 minutes or until tender. Cool and refrigerate in remaining liquid. Drain and serve.

Nutritional Data

PER SERVING				EXCHANGES			
Calories:	25	Cholesterol (mg):	0	Milk: 0.0		Bread: 0.0	
Fat (gm):	.1	Sodium (mg):	2.9	Veg.: 0.4		Meat: 0.0	
Sat. fat (gm):	0	% Calories from fat:	2	Fruit: 0.0		Fat: 0.3	

MYKONOS MUSHROOM SOUP

Yield: 3 cups

1 medium onion
1 cup low-sodium chicken bouillon
2 cups low-sodium tomato juice
1 lb. fresh mushrooms, sliced
1 teaspoon **Savory Tarragon Blend**

Saute onion in bouillon in a 3-quart, non-stick saucepan. Add tomato juice and Savory Tarragon Blend and simmer for 30 minutes, stirring occasionally. Add mushrooms and simmer for 15 minutes more.

Nutritional Data

PER CUP				EXCHANGES			
Calories:	80	Cholesterol (mg):	0	Milk: 0.0		Bread: 0.0	
Fat (gm):	1.1	Sodium (mg):	250	Veg.: 3.2		Meat: 0.0	
Sat. fat (gm):	.1	% Calories from fat:	7	Fruit: 0.0		Fat: 0.0	

19.
HOT
SPICE
BLENDS

♦

Cajun Blend
5-Alarm Hot Stuff Blend
Southwestern Fire Blend
Zippy Pepper Blend
Jamaican Scorcher Blend

♦

Cajun Blend

1 Tablespoon chili powder
1 Tablespoon paprika
1 Tablespoon onion flakes
1 Tablespoon garlic powder
1 Tablespoon allspice
1 Tablespoon cayenne pepper
1 Tablespoon thyme

Skinny Spices Tip

Use allspice with soups, seafood, poultry, and fruit salads. Its scent will make you think of a blend of cinnamon, cloves, and nutmeg.

VOODOO QUEEN VEGETABLES

Yield: 4 servings

2 medium zucchini
10 ounces canned tomatoes
1 small green onion or dehydrated equivalent
½ stalk celery
¼ green pepper
  Sugar substitute to taste
  Salt substitute to taste
  Pepper to taste
½ teaspoon **Cajun Blend**

Wash zucchini, cut ends off, and cut into 1-inch pieces. Put into saucepan with all remaining ingredients. Cook over low heat, uncovered, until tender.

Nutritional Data

PER SERVING				EXCHANGES			
Calories:	18	Cholesterol (mg):	0	Milk:	0.0	Bread:	0.0
Fat (gm):	.2	Sodium (mg):	129	Veg.:	0.7	Meat:	0.0
Sat. fat (gm):	0	% Calories from fat:	9	Fruit:	0.0	Fat:	0.0

FRENCH MARKET TOMATO SOUP

Yield: 2 servings

12 ounces no-salt-added tomato juice
1 small clove garlic, mashed
1 Tablespoon red onion
2 Tablespoons parsley, chopped
1 Tablespoon wine vinegar
½ package low-sodium beef bouillon
¼ teaspoon **Cajun Blend**
  Pepper to taste

Put garlic and onion into food processor and liquefy. Add all other ingredients and process for 2–3 minutes. Serve hot or cold with cucumber slices.

Nutritional Data

PER SERVING				EXCHANGES			
Calories:	48	Cholesterol (mg):	0	Milk:	0.0	Bread:	0.0
Fat (gm):	.3	Sodium (mg):	270	Veg.:	2.0	Meat:	0.0
Sat. fat (gm):	0	% Calories from fat:	4	Fruit:	0.0	Fat:	0.0

5-ALARM HOT STUFF

1 Tablespoon granulated garlic
1 Tablespoon onion flakes
1 Tablespoon red pepper flakes
½ Tablespoon ground ginger
½ Tablespoon thyme
½ Tablespoon mustard powder
½ Tablespoon ground cloves
½ Tablespoon coarsely ground black
   pepper
½ Tablespoon paprika
½ Tablespoon cumin
1 teaspoon bay leaf
1 teaspoon parsley flakes

Skinny Spices Tip

For a quick hot-and-spicy herb blend, combine basil, bay, oregano,
parsley, and red pepper flakes.

VEGETABLES FROM HELL

Yield: 6 servings

½ cup dried shitake mushrooms
1 cup celery, sliced
1 7-ounce package frozen pea pods
1 teaspoon low-sodium soy sauce
½ teaspoon **5-Alarm Hot Stuff**

Pour warm water over mushrooms to cover, and let sit for 20 minutes to soften. Drain and slice. Cook celery in salted water for 5 minutes. Cook pea pods as directed on package. Toss all vegetables together with soy sauce and 5-Alarm Hot Stuff.

Nutritional Data

PER SERVING				EXCHANGES			
Calories:	76	Cholesterol (mg):	0	Milk:	0.0	Bread:	0.0
Fat (gm):	.3	Sodium (mg):	40.5	Veg.:	3.0	Meat:	0.0
Sat. fat (gm):	.1	% Calories from fat:	4	Fruit:	0.0	Fat:	0.0

HOTSY TOTSY MUSTARD DRESSING

Yield: 8 servings

1 Tablespoon prepared mustard
2 Tablespoons lemon juice
⅛ teaspoon **5-Alarm Hot Stuff**
⅔ cup non-fat skim milk powder
⅔ cup water
½ teaspoon salt substitute
   Dash freshly ground pepper
½ teaspoon sugar substitute

Blend all ingredients together and store in fridge.

Nutritional Data

PER SERVING				EXCHANGES			
Calories:	23	Cholesterol (mg):	1	Milk:	0.2	Bread:	0.0
Fat (gm):	.1	Sodium (mg):	55.6	Veg.:	0.0	Meat:	0.0
Sat. fat (gm):	0	% Calories from fat:	5	Fruit:	0.0	Fat:	0.0

SOUTHWESTERN FIRE

1 Tablespoon granulated onion
1 Tablespoon paprika
1 Tablespoon chili powder
1 Tablespoon cumin
½ Tablespoon garlic
½ Tablespoon cayenne pepper
½ Tablespoon ground coriander
½ Tablespoon oregano
½ Tablespoon dried lemon peel

Skinny Spices Tip

Cumin adds an especially delightful accent to yogurt-based dishes and dips.

SANTA FE DRESSING

Yield: 8 servings

8 ounces buttermilk
2 teaspoons horseradish
¼ teaspoon **Southwestern Fire**
¼ teaspoon salt substitute
1 teaspoon minced onion

Combine all ingredients; blend well and refrigerate.

Nutritional Data

PER SERVING				EXCHANGES			
Calories:	12	Cholesterol (mg):	1	Milk:	0.1	Bread:	0.0
Fat (gm):	.3	Sodium (mg):	31	Veg.:	0.0	Meat:	0.0
Sat. fat (gm):	.2	% Calories from fat:	19	Fruit:	0.0	Fat:	0.0

LIQUID DYNAMITE CRAB BISQUE

Yield: 2 servings

2 cups skim milk
1 stalk celery, cut up
1 small onion or equivalent, dehydrated
1 bay leaf
½ teaspoon salt substitute
½ teaspoon **Southwestern Fire**
8 ounces frozen crab meat
Minced parsley

Heat milk with celery, onions, and bay leaf. Strain after simmering for 15 minutes. Stir together seasoned milk, salt, and Southwestern Fire. Add frozen crab meat. Simmer over low heat until crab thaws and separates, stirring frequently. Garnish with minced parsley.

Nutritional Data

PER SERVING				EXCHANGES			
Calories:	215	Cholesterol (mg):	118	Milk:	1.0	Bread:	0.0
Fat (gm):	31.7	Sodium (mg):	460	Veg.:	0.6	Meat:	2.5
Sat. fat (gm):	2.5	% Calories from fat:	11	Fruit:	0.0	Fat:	0.0

ZIPPY PEPPER BLEND

1 Tablespoon black pepper
1 Tablespoon thyme
1 Tablespoon marjoram
1 Tablespoon tarragon
1 Tablespoon basil
1 Tablespoon dried chives
1 Tablespoon hot red pepper flakes

Skinny Spices Tip

Try seasoning your next low-calorie Mexican dish with a combination of chili pepper, fresh cilantro, oregano, garlic, and lime juice.

VERY SPECIAL CREAMY PEPPER DRESSING

Yield: 8 servings

1 Tablespoon no-salt-added tomato juice
½ teaspoon oregano
½ teaspoon marjoram
½ teaspoon paprika
½ teaspoon **Zippy Pepper Blend**
¼ teaspoon dry mustard
½ clove garlic, pureed
1 cup buttermilk

Mix all seasonings and tomato juice. Add buttermilk and mix well.

Nutritional Data

PER SERVING

				EXCHANGES			
Calories:	15	Cholesterol (mg):	1.1	Milk:	0.1	Bread:	0.0
Fat (gm):	.3	Sodium (mg):	32.7	Veg.:	0.0	Meat:	0.0
Sat. fat (gm):	.2	% Calories from fat:	19	Fruit:	0.0	Fat:	0.0

SINFUL CREAMED MUSHROOMS

Yield: 1 serving

1 slice low-calorie bread
2 ounces low-fat cottage cheese
2 ounces canned mushrooms
1 packet low-sodium chicken bouillon
¼ teaspoon **Zippy Pepper Blend**

Toast one side of bread and place toasted side down on aluminum foil. Combine all other ingredients. Heap on bread. Broil until cottage cheese is melted and slightly brown.

Nutritional Data

PER SERVING

				EXCHANGES			
Calories:	99	Cholesterol (mg):	2.5	Milk:	0.0	Bread:	0.5
Fat (gm):	1.3	Sodium (mg):	568	Veg.:	0.7	Meat:	0.0
Sat. fat (gm):	.5	% Calories from fat:	13	Fruit:	0.0	Fat:	0.0

JAMAICAN SCORCHER BLEND

1 Tablespoon ground ginger
1 Tablespoon mustard seed
1 Tablespoon granulated onion
½ Tablespoon allspice
½ Tablespoon granulated garlic
½ Tablespoon paprika
½ Tablespoon thyme
½ Tablespoon dried lemon peel
½ Tablespoon coarsely ground black pepper
½ Tablespoon hot red pepper flakes
½ Tablespoon ground cloves

Skinny Spices Tip

To create interesting low-calorie mustard blends, combine mustard powder with wine, beer, or even skimmed milk. Add extra flavor with marjoram, tarragon, chervil, or chives.

KINGSTON KILLER DRESSING

Yield: 12 servings

1 cup plain low-fat yogurt
½ cup chili sauce
¼–½ teaspoon **Jamaican Scorcher Blend**
(depending on your pain threshold)

Blend thoroughly and chill. Great with exotic veggies such as jicama or steamed baby zucchini.

Nutritional Data

PER SERVING				EXCHANGES			
Calories:	15	Cholesterol (mg):	1.2	Milk: 0.1		Bread: 0.0	
Fat (gm):	.4	Sodium (mg):	16.9	Veg.: 0.1		Meat: 0.0	
Sat. fat (gm):	.2	% Calories from fat:	22	Fruit: 0.0		Fat: 0.0	

OCHOS RIOS HADDOCK

Yield: 4 servings

1 pound haddock fillet
1 lemon, seeded and cut up with peel
½ clove garlic
1 stalk celery, diced
1 Tablespoon Worcestershire sauce
1 teaspoon oregano
1 teaspoon parsley flakes
1 teaspoon horseradish
½ teaspoon **Jamaican Scorcher Blend**

Put all ingredients except fish into blender and chop well for about 15 seconds. Cut fish into individual servings and wrap in foil. Before closing foil, spoon chopped mixture evenly over fish. Close tightly and bake in preheated oven at 325° for 45 minutes.

Nutritional Data

PER SERVING				EXCHANGES			
Calories:	108	Cholesterol (mg):	64.6	Milk: 0.0		Bread: 0.0	
Fat (gm):	.9	Sodium (mg):	129	Veg.: 0.1		Meat: 4.0	
Sat. fat (gm):	.2	% Calories from fat:	7	Fruit: 0.2		Fat: 0.0	

20.
SWEET SPICE BLENDS

◆

Baker's Choice Blend
Sweet Treat Blend
Choc-o-holic Blend
Indian Dessert Blend
Apple & Pumpkin Pie Blend
Ginger Snap Blend
Citrus Cooler Blend

◆

Baker's Choice Blend

2 Tablespoons ground cinnamon
1½ Tablespoons ground ginger
1½ Tablespoons ground nutmeg
1 Tablespoon dried lemon peel
1 Tablespoon ground cloves

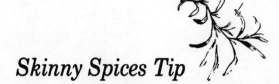

Skinny Spices Tip

Spices can add a new dimension to fruit desserts and make them seem extra-special:

apples with cinnamon
peaches with ginger
pears with clove
oranges with cinnamon or clove
sliced grapes with allspice or nutmeg

GUILT-FREE APPLE PIE

Yield: 4 servings

4 apples, peeled, cored, and sliced
1 12-ounce can low-calorie lemon-lime soda
1 package unflavored gelatin
Sweetener (equal to 4 teaspoons sugar)
⅓ cup dry non-fat milk
½ teaspoon **Baker's Choice Blend**

Dissolve sugar substitute in gelatin, and ½ of the dry milk in lemon-lime soda. Arrange apples in 8-inch cake pan. Spoon liquid over it carefully. Sprinkle remainder of dry milk over top and dust with Baker's Choice Blend. Bake in 350° oven for 1 hour. Cool and refrigerate.

Nutritional Data

PER SERVING				EXCHANGES			
Calories:	143	Cholesterol (mg):	1	Milk:	0.2	Bread:	0.0
Fat (gm):	.5	Sodium (mg):	39.8	Veg.:	0.0	Meat:	0.1
Sat. fat (gm):	.1	% Calories from fat:	3	Fruit:	2.1	Fat:	0.0

PINEAPPLE FROZEN SOLIDS

Yield: 2 servings

16 ounces buttermilk
4 ounces unsweetened crushed pineapple
1 Tablespoon sugar substitute (or more to taste)
⅛ teaspoon **Baker's Choice Blend**

Mix all ingredients together and spill into an ice cube tray. Put in coldest part of your freezer for 1½ hours. Pop out and enjoy!

Nutritional Data

PER SERVING				EXCHANGES			
Calories:	126	Cholesterol (mg):	7.9	Milk:	1.0	Bread:	0.0
Fat (gm):	2	Sodium (mg):	238	Veg.:	0.0	Meat:	0.0
Sat. fat (gm):	1.2	% Calories from fat:	14	Fruit:	0.6	Fat:	0.0

SWEET TREAT BLEND

2½ Tablespoons ground nutmeg
2½ Tablespoons ground vanilla bean
2 Tablespoons powdered or granular
sugar substitute

Skinny Spices Tip

Indulge in Skinny Cinnamon Toast: toast low-calorie bread in oven or
toaster, sprinkle powdered sugar substitute plus **Sweet Treat Blend** on
bread, and then toast again. A few drops of skim milk brushed over the
bread before sprinkling will help the sweetener adhere to the surface.

KNOCKOUT SWEET ROLL

Yield: 4 servings

6 ounces farmer or ricotta cheese

1 large egg

1 capful vanilla

Sugar substitute equal to 6 teaspoons of sugar (or to taste)

⅛ teaspoon **Sweet Treat Blend**

3 Tablespoons crushed pineapple or fresh peaches

2 pieces low-calorie bread, toasted and divided into quarters

Mix first five ingredients with a fork, and spread half on each slice of bread. Spread crushed pineapple or peach bits on top, and broil until lightly browned.

Nutritional Data

PER SERVING				EXCHANGES			
Calories:	110	Cholesterol (mg):	66.1	Milk: 0.0		Bread: 0.3	
Fat (gm):	5	Sodium (mg):	132	Veg.: 0.0		Meat: 0.9	
Sat. fat (gm):	2.5	% Calories from fat:	40	Fruit: 0.1		Fat: 0.6	

TROPICAL NIGHTS BREAD PUDDING

Yield: 2 servings

1 cup skim milk

Liquid egg substitute to equal 1 egg

Liquid sugar substitute to equal 6 teaspoons sugar

½ teaspoon coconut extract

½ teaspoon pineapple extract

½ teaspoon vanilla extract

1½ slices 40-calorie white or wheat bread, cubed

Sweet Treat Blend to taste

Combine all ingredients except bread and Sweet Treat Blend in the blender or food processor and process until frothy. Pour mixture into small baking dish, and press bread cubes into mixture to soak up liquid. Sprinkle with Sweet Treat Blend to taste. Place baking dish in a pan with ½ inch of very hot tap water. Bake at 350° for 50 minutes, until knife comes out clean. Eat hot or cold.

Nutritional Data

PER SERVING				EXCHANGES			
Calories:	102	Cholesterol (mg):	2.3	Milk: 0.5		Bread: 0.5	
Fat (gm):	1.2	Sodium (mg):	151	Veg.: 0.0		Meat: 0.1	
Sat. fat (gm):	.3	% Calories from fat:	10	Fruit: 0.1		Fat: 0.1	

Choc-o-holic Blend

3 Tablespoons unsweetened cocoa powder
3 Tablespoons powdered or granular
   sugar substitute
1 Tablespoon cinnamon

Skinny Spices Tip

Add a dash of cinnamon to your next batch of spaghetti sauce, and liven up an old Italian favorite.

THICK AND CREAMY CHOCOLATE LOVER'S SHAKE

Yield: 1 serving

- 1 cup skim milk
- 1 teaspoon chocolate extract
- ¼ teaspoon **Choc-o-holic Blend**
- ½ teaspoon instant decaffeinated coffee
- 4–5 ice cubes

Place all ingredients in blender for about 30 seconds. Add additional ice cube if extra thickness is desired.

Nutritional Data

PER SERVING				EXCHANGES			
Calories:	101	Cholesterol (mg):	4.4	Milk:	1.0	Bread:	0.0
Fat (gm):	.4	Sodium (mg):	126	Veg.:	0.0	Meat:	0.0
Sat. fat (gm):	.3	% Calories from fat:	4	Fruit:	0.1	Fat:	0.2

CHOCOLATE RUM CUSTARD

Yield: 1 serving

- 4 ounces undiluted evaporated skim milk
- ½ teaspoon rum extract
- ½ teaspoon vanilla extract
- 1 teaspoon **Choc-o-holic Blend**
- ¾ teaspoon liquid sugar substitute
- 8 large ice cubes

Place all ingredients except ice into blender. Start blender and add ice one cube at a time. When mixture reaches the consistency of frozen custard, spoon into chilled glasses.

Nutritional Data

PER SERVING				EXCHANGES			
Calories:	106	Cholesterol (mg):	4.1	Milk:	0.9	Bread:	0.0
Fat (gm):	.4	Sodium (mg):	131	Veg.:	0.0	Meat:	0.0
Sat. fat (gm):	.2	% Calories from fat:	4	Fruit:	0.1	Fat:	0.2

INDIAN DESSERT BLEND

2 Tablespoons ground cardamon
2 Tablespoons allspice
2 Tablespoons cinnamon
1 Tablespoon powdered or granular sugar
  substitute

Skinny Spices Tip

Try Tropical Whip for a light, elegant dessert: dissolve 1 package of
artificially sweetened orange gelatin in 12 ounces of boiling ginger ale.
Add 4 ounces cold orange juice and ⅛ teaspoon **Indian Dessert Blend.**
Chill until just slightly thickened, then whip until fluffy. Spoon into
1-quart mold or individual molds. Chill until firm. Unmold and serve.

COCONUT APPLE CRUNCH COOKIES

Yield: 20 cookies

- ¾ cup grated apple
- 6 Tablespoons brown sugar substitute
- ½ teaspoon coconut extract or vanilla extract
- ½ teaspoon **Indian Dessert Blend**
- 1⅓ cup non-fat dry milk (powder form)

Mix all ingredients in mixing bowl. Drop by teaspoonfuls onto non-stick cookie sheet or cookie sheet sprayed with non-stick spray. Bake in 350° oven for approximately 15 minutes. Store in tightly covered container.

Nutritional Data

PER COOKIE				EXCHANGES			
Calories:	23	Cholesterol (mg):	.8	Milk: 0.2	Bread: 0.0
Fat (gm):	.1	Sodium (mg):	27	Veg.: 0.0	Meat: 0.0
Sat. fat (gm):	0	% Calories from fat:	2	Fruit: 0.1	Fat: 0.0

FAKE RICE PUDDING

Yield: 2 servings

- 1 small package frozen cauliflower
  Sugar substitute to taste
- ¼ cup skim milk
- ⅛ teaspoon **Indian Dessert Blend**
  Dash of cinnamon

Cook cauliflower until extremely well done. Drain and mash or food process to a medium consistency. Add sweetener, Indian Dessert Blend, and milk. Place in custard cups and sprinkle with a light dash of cinnamon.

Nutritional Data

PER SERVING				EXCHANGES			
Calories:	37	Cholesterol (mg):	.6	Milk: 0.1	Bread: 0.0
Fat (gm):	.6	Sodium (mg):	32.8	Veg.: 1.8	Meat: 0.0
Sat. fat (gm):	.1	% Calories from fat:	12	Fruit: 0.0	Fat: 0.0

APPLE & PUMPKIN PIE BLEND

4 Tablespoons cinnamon
2 Tablespoons ground nutmeg
1 Tablespoon ground cloves

Skinny Spices Tip

Sink your teeth into a Skinny Spices Cheese Danish. Toast one slice of 40-calorie bread lightly, and top with 2 ounces of low-fat cottage cheese. Sprinkle with **Apple & Pumpkin Pie Blend** and powdered or granular sugar substitute, and place under broiler for 3 to 4 minutes.

BUBBLING BROWN SUGAR PEACHES

Yield: 2 servings

4 fresh peaches
4 teaspoons brown sugar substitute
1 teaspoon **Apple & Pumpkin Pie Blend**

Skin, pit, and halve peaches. Sprinkle with brown sugar substitute and Apple & Pumpkin Pie Blend. Bake at 300° for 10 minutes, then put under broiler for a few minutes to brown slightly.

Nutritional Data

PER SERVING				EXCHANGES			
Calories:	100	Cholesterol (mg):	0	Milk: 0.0	Bread· 0.0
Fat (gm):	.2	Sodium (mg):	4.8	Veg.: 0.0	Meat: 0.0
Sat. fat (gm):	0	% Calories from fat:	2	Fruit: 5.2	Fat: 0.0

BERRY SPECIAL YOGURT DESSERT

Yield: 2 servings

1 cup plain low-fat yogurt
½ cup strawberries
1½ teaspoon liquid sugar substitute
1 teaspoon vanilla
½ teaspoon **Apple & Pumpkin Pie Blend**

Combine all ingredients and chill thoroughly.

Nutritional Data

PER SERVING				EXCHANGES			
Calories:	95	Cholesterol (mg):	7.5	Milk: 0.7	Bread: 0.0
Fat (gm):	2	Sodium (mg):	86.4	Veg.: 0.0	Meat: 0.0
Sat. fat (gm):	1	% Calories from fat:	20	Fruit: 0.2	Fat: 0.4

GINGER SNAP BLEND

4 Tablespoons ground ginger
2 Tablespoons ground nutmeg
1 Tablespoon ground cloves

Skinny Spices Tip

For a change of pace at breakfast, try Skinny Spices French Toast. Soak
1 slice of 40-calorie bread in a well-beaten egg. Broil on foil. Sprinkle
Ginger Snap Blend on top.

HOLIDAY PUMPKIN CUSTARD

Yield: 4 servings

1 cup canned low-sodium pumpkin
1 cup reconstituted dry non-fat milk
2 eggs
   Liquid or powdered sweetener equal to ¼ cup
   sugar
½ teaspoon vanilla
¾ teaspoon cinnamon
⅓ teaspoon **Ginger Snap Blend**

In large mixing bowl, beat all ingredients together until well blended. Pour into 4, 6-ounce custard cups and bake in preheated 350° oven 50 minutes or until knife inserted in center comes out clean.

Nutritional Data

PER SERVING				EXCHANGES			
Calories:	45	Cholesterol (mg):	1.1	Milk: 0.2	Bread: 0.3
Fat (gm):	.3	Sodium (mg):	34.7	Veg.: 0.0	Meat: 0.0
Sat. fat (gm):	.2	% Calories from fat:	6	Fruit: 0.0	Fat: 0.0

ORIENTAL ICED MELON BALLS

Yield: 6 servings

1 honeydew melon
2 Tablespoons lime juice
½ teaspoon **Ginger Snap Blend**

Ball honeydew melon, sprinkle with lime juice, and dust with Ginger Snap Blend. Serve ice cold.

Nutritional Data

PER SERVING				EXCHANGES			
Calories:	77	Cholesterol (mg):	0	Milk: 0.0	Bread: 0.0
Fat (gm):	.2	Sodium (mg):	21.6	Veg.: 0.0	Meat: 0.0
Sat. fat (gm):	0	% Calories from fat:	2	Fruit: 1.3	Fat: 0.0

CITRUS COOLER BLEND

4 Tablespoons Kool Aid Unsweetened
   Lemon Drink Mix
3 Tablespoons granulated sugar substitute

Skinny Spices Tip

Experiment with individual spices that can add a new dimension to
sweet recipes: allspice, anise, cardamon, cinnamon, cloves, fennel, lemon
peel, ginger, mace, nutmeg, mint, orange peel, and rosemary.

DIETER'S FROZEN DAIQUIRI

Yield: 1 serving

- 2 ounces lime juice
- 4 ounces water
- 1–2 teaspoons **Citrus Cooler Blend** to taste
- 1 teaspoon rum extract

Blend above ingredients with ice in blender until slushy. Garnish with twist of lime or lemon and serve.

Nutritional Data

PER SERVING				EXCHANGES			
Calories:	26	Cholesterol (mg):	0	Milk: 0.0	Bread:	0.0
Fat (gm):	.1	Sodium (mg):	2	Veg.: 0.0	Meat:	0.0
Sat. fat (gm):	0	% Calories from fat:	2	Fruit: 0.3	Fat:	0.1

CHERRY ITALIAN ICES

Yield: 1 large serving

- 3 ounces water
- 1 teaspoon Kool Aid unsweetened cherry flavor
- 1 teaspoon **Citrus Cooler Blend**
  Extra sweetener to taste
- 1–1½ cups crushed ice cubes

Mix all ingredients together and freeze until firm. Place in blender for 30–45 seconds for slushy cherry Italian ices.

Nutritional Data

PER SERVING				EXCHANGES			
Calories:	11	Cholesterol (mg):	0	Milk: 0.0	Bread:	0.0
Fat (gm):	0	Sodium (mg):	1.4	Veg.: 0.0	Meat:	0.0
Sat. fat (gm):	0	% Calories from fat:	.1	Fruit: 0.1	Fat:	0.0

21.
BLAH BUSTERS: BRAND-NAME SUBSTITUTES FOR HIGH-CALORIE FOODS

I t's not surprising that most people think about dieting in terms of giving up their favorite foods. Bidding a fond farewell to pizza . . . sadly licking their last ice cream cone . . . skipping the creamy salad dressings . . . or tossing out the brownies. No wonder just the thought of dieting is enough to make you plunge head first into the refrigerator! Deprivation is the chief enemy of any dieter and can undermine even the most determined weight-loss effort.

It's been my experience that you stand a far better chance of being a successful dieter if you think *first* of the foods you love and then concentrate on finding lower-calorie substitutes that may be equally satisfying. (Then again, you may not find a good substitute, but at least you've become familiar with some of the alternatives.) Fortunately, more and more supermarkets are stocking healthier food choices, and dozens of new calorie-reduced products arrive on the shelves every day. What's more, food technology has improved to such a degree that most of these products successfully mimic their higher-calorie cousins and really can fool the taste buds.

Below are just some of the excellent brand-name, low-calorie substitutes that have helped me stay sane while fighting the battle of the bulge.

Alcohol

Instead of regular white wine at 80 calories per 4 ounces, try *Almaden Light Chablis* at 61 calories per 4 ounces.

Instead of regular rose wine at 88 calories per 4 ounces, try *Masson Light Premium Rose* at 64 calories per 4 ounces.

Dairy Items

Instead of regular butter or margarine at 100 calories per Tablespoon, try *Weight Watcher's Diet Margarine* in salted and unsalted varieties for 50 calories per Tablespoon.

Instead of diet margarine at 50 calories per Tablespoon, try *Butter Buds Sprinkles* at 4 calories per ½ teaspoon or *Weight Watcher's Butter-Flavored Spray* at 2 calories per spray.

Instead of Philadelphia Cream Cheese at 100 calories per ounce, try *Philadelphia Light* at 60 calories per ounce.

Instead of regular sour cream at 31 calories per Tablespoon, try *Molly McButter Sour Cream Sprinkles* at 8 calories per teaspoon.

Instead of Dannon regular Fruit Yogurt at 240 calories per cup, try *Dannon Light Yogurt* at 100 calories per cup.

Instead of regular half-and-half at 50 calories per Tablespoon, try *Non-Dairy Mocha Mix* at 20 calories per Tablespoon.

Desserts

Instead of regular high-butterfat, premium ice creams such as Haagen Dazs at 250–310 calories per 4 ounces, try *Simple Pleasures* ice cream in flavors like rum raisin, toffee crunch, chocolate, and strawberry at 110–140 per 3 ounces; or *Baskin Robbins Lite* in flavors like banana, chocolate mint, or jamoca almond at 110–130 calories per 4 ounces. For even fewer calories try *Baskin Robbins Sugar Free Ice Cream*, with only 80–100 calories per 4 ounces.

Instead of a regular brownie at 170 calories, try a *Weight Watcher's Brownie* at 100 calories.

Instead of regular cheesecake at 280 calories per slice, try *Weight Watcher's Strawberry Cheesecake* at 180 calories per slice, or *Weight Watcher's Brownie Cheesecake* at 200 calories per slice.

Instead of a regular slice of cinnamon Danish at 150 calories, try a slice of *Entemman's Light Cinnamon Twist* for 80 calories.

Instead of Reese's Peanut Butter Cups at 240 calories for 2, try *Weight Watcher's Frozen Peanut Butter Bars* at 60 calories per bar, or *Edy's Grand Light Peanut Butter and Chocolate Dairy Dessert* at 140 calories per ½ cup.

Instead of regular chocolate cupcakes at 170 calories each, try *Hostess Light Chocolate Cupcakes* at 110 calories each.

Instead of a slice of regular double-crust apple pie at 404 calories, try a *Weight Watcher's Apple Sweet Roll* at 190 calories.

Instead of Jello Regular Chocolate Pudding at 180 calories per ½ cup, try *Jello Sugar-Free Pudding* at 90 calories per ½ cup.

Instead of regular chocolate mousse at 754 calories per cup, try *Weight Watcher's Chocolate Flavor Mousse* at 120 calories per cup.

Instead of regular Extra Creamy Cool Whip for 14 calories per Tablespoon, try *Cool Whip Lite* at 8 calories per Tablespoon.

Instead of 2 regular oatmeal raisin cookies at 160 calories, try 2 *Entemman's Light Oatmeal Raisin Cookies* for 80 calories.

Instead of Jello Regular Gelatin at 80 calories per ½ cup, try *Jello Sugar-Free Gelatin* at 8 calories per ½ cup.

Jams, Jellies, Syrups, and Condiments

Instead of regular ketchup at 18 calories per Tablespoon, try *Heinz Lite Ketchup* at 8 calories per Tablespoon.

Instead of regular jam at 18 calories per teaspoon, try *Smucker's Low Sugar Jams* at 8 calories per teaspoon.

Instead of regular Aunt Jemima Syrup at 110 calories per 2 Tablespoons, try *Aunt Jemima Lite* at 50 calories per 2 Tablespoons.

Mayonnaise and Salad Dressings

Instead of Kraft regular mayonnaise at 100 calories per Tablespoon, try *Kraft Light Reduced Calorie Mayonnaise* at 50 calories per Tablespoon.

Instead of regular ranch dressing at 50–60 calories per Tablespoon, try *Good Seasons Lite Ranch* at 30 calories per Tablespoon.

Instead of regular Italian dressing at 80 calories per Tablespoon, try *Kraft Oil Free Italian Dressing* at 4 calories per Tablespoon.

Instead of regular blue cheese dressing at 77 calories per Tablespoon, try *Wishbone Lite Chunky Blue Cheese* at 40 calories per Tablespoon.

Meat, Fish, and Cheese

Instead of regular hot dogs at 150 calories per frank, try *Louis Rich Turkey Dogs* at 100 calories per frank.

Instead of regular tuna in oil at 150 calories per 2 ounces, try *Bumble Bee Solid White Tuna in Water* at 70 calories per 2 ounces.

Instead of regular cheese at 100 calories per slice, try *Weight Watcher's Cheese* at 50 calories per slice in American or sharp Cheddar; or *Lifetime Natural Cheese* in mild Cheddar, Monterey Jack, mozzarella, Swiss, and Muenster at 50 calories per slice.

Instead of regular Kentucky Fried Chicken at 463 calories for a 2-piece snack dinner, try *Weight Watcher's Southern Fried Chicken Patty Dinner* at 340 calories.

Instead of regular beef stroganoff at 390 calories, try *Armour Classics Lite Beef Stroganoff* at 250 calories.

Instead of a regular Salisbury steak dinner at 500 calories, try *Healthy Choice Salisbury Steak Dinner* at 300 calories.

Instead of regular ham at 50 calories per slice, try *Louis Rich Turkey Ham* at 35 calories per slice.

Instead of regular bologna at 90 calories per slice, try *Louis Rich Turkey Bologna* at 60 calories per slice.

Snacks

Instead of regular French bread sausage pizza at 840 calories, try *Lean Cuisine Sausage French Bread Pizza* at 330 calories.

Instead of 15 regular Doritos chips at 140 calories, try 15 *Doritos Lite* chips at 110 calories.

Soups, Bouillons, and Cocoas

Instead of high-sodium chicken or beef bouillon at 90 mgs sodium, try *Herb Ox* chicken or beef bouillon packets with 5 mg sodium. The low- and high-sodium varieties both contain 8 calories.

Instead of regular cream of broccoli soup at 210 calories per 6 ounces, try *Lipton Lite Cup a Soup* at 40 calories per 6 ounces.

Instead of regular hot chocolate at 110 calories per 8 ounces, try *Carnation Sugar Free Hot Chocolate* at 50 calories per 8 ounces.

Sugar and Baking Ingredients

Instead of Pet Regular Evaporated Milk at 170 calories per ½ cup, try *Pet Light Evaporated Milk* at 100 calories per ½ cup.

Instead of regular brown sugar for 16 calories per teaspoon, try *Sugar Twin Brown Sugar Replacement* at 1½ calories per teaspoon.

Instead of regular white sugar for 10 calories per teaspoon, try *Equal®* for 4 calories per packet (equals 2 teaspoons of sugar); or 10 drops of any *liquid sweetener* at 0 calories per teaspoon.

22.
YOUR MAIL ORDER GUIDE TO SPICES

A lthough it's more convenient to buy your whole or ground spices locally, I know that not everyone's supermarket carries an extensive array of spices, and many people don't live near a gourmet store that carries some of the more exotic selections. The following catalog firms have been reliable sources for mail order spices as well as for unusual condiments that can help add zip to any diet meal.

Adriana's Bazaar
2152 Broadway at 75th Street
New York, NY 10023
(212) 877-5757 – Phone
(212) 877-5760 – FAX

A spicy newcomer to the mail-order scene, Adriana's specializes in exotic spices from India, Mexico, the Middle East, and Europe. Adriana's is the best choice for chili peppers, Moroccan berbere, and Indonesian seeni sambal. It's also the ultimate international food source for vanilla beans, tandoori chicken spices, and Thai holy basil.

Cinnabar Specialty Foods
1134 W. Haining Street
Prescott, AZ 86301
(800) 824-4563 or
(602) 778-3687

Cinnabar's specialty is Indian chutneys—flavorful combinations of fruits, vegetables, and spices. I always keep a jar of their superb Tomato Chutney on hand for chicken, fish, or vegetables, but my husband is equally enamored of the pear-cardamon variety.

Dilijan Liquid Spice
Dilijan Products, Inc.
P.O. Box 145
Ringoes, NJ 08551
(201) 806-6048

This is a revolutionary new product—spices in liquid form with a two-year shelf life. Dilijan Liquid Spice is a one-to-one replacement for dried seasonings, but the flavor is absolutely garden-fresh. Available in Basil, Onion, Garlic, Dill, Chili, Hot Red Pepper, Oregano, Thyme, Curry, Clove, and Sage. The Basil is especially outstanding. All flavors are available by mail; send for their price list.

Dried Herbs from Nature's Wonderland
Penn Herb Company
603 N. 2nd Street
Philadelphia, PA 19123
(215) 925-3336

Stocks more than 500 herb varieties, teas, folk remedies, and books. And their catalog costs just $1.

The Gourmet Gardener
4000 W. 126th Street
Leawood, KS 66209
(913) 345-0490

If you'd rather grow your own herbs and spices instead of picking them off a supermarket shelf, The Gourmet Gardener is a great start. In addition to a full array of culinary herbs, the catalog offers seeds for exotic vegetables, greens, and edible flowers. Also a good selection of gardening books for traditional and container gardens.

The Herbfarm Armchair Sampler
32804 Issaquah-Fall City Road
Fall City, WA 98024
(206) 784-2222

The Herbfarm offers hundreds of herb varieties and herbal gifts through their 35-page catalog. In addition, the owners publish a bimonthly magazine called *The Herb Companion* for herb lovers, gardeners, and cooks for $21 a year. The catalog is free; a sample issue of the magazine costs $4.

House of Spices
76-17 Broadway
Jackson Heights, NY 11373
(718) 476-1577

This homegrown catalog brings an Indian spice bazaar right to your doorstep. You'll find exotic spices such as fenugreek (mentioned in the "Indian Spice Blends" section), powdered fennel seeds, whole nutmeg, and sanchal (black salt) not to mention tongue twisters like calonji, methi barhdo, and pani puri masala.

Island Imports
P.O. Box 78925
Los Angeles, CA 90016
(213) 732-6320

Island Imports is the home of Evadney's All Purpose Jamaican Hot Sauce, one of the best, most fiery hot sauces in the country and a superb accompaniment for cottage cheese or even plain rice. Even the mild variety is pretty incendiary, but if you love "hot and spicy," this will rearrange your taste buds.

The Kitchen Shop
The Phoenix Building
670 Higuera Street
San Luis Obispo, CA 93401
(805) 541-0225

If for some reason I haven't been able to convince you by now that whipping up your own spice blends is fun and easy, you may want to cheat a little and send for a complete listing of Spice Hunter blends available through the Kitchen Shop of San Luis Obispo, California. These salt-free, sugar-free, all-natural-spice blends come in delectable varieties such as Thai, Cajun/Creole, Fajita, Spicy Island Bean, Szechuan, and Pesto. The service at the Kitchen Shop is first-rate, and most spice blends cost just $2 to $4. Spice Hunter blends will even make your kitchen smell extra inviting when you're *not* cooking!

Madeline's Gourmet Kitchen
P.O. Box 1302
Atascadero, CA 93423
(805) 461-4809

Here's another way to cheat if you don't want to mix up *Skinny Spices* blends yourself. Madeline's offers a staggering variety of salt- and preservatives-free seasoning blends, individual spices, and peppercorns. Plus, you'll receive a free sample when you order the $1 catalog.

The Mail Order Spice House, Ltd.
P.O. Box 1633
Milwaukee, WI 53201
(414) 768-8799

This is the most complete purveyor of mail-order spices and herbs in America. They even make their own marvelous salt-free blends, including Sunny Spain Seasoning, a fragrant lemon-pepper combination. Mail Order Spice House is a good source for specialized items you may not be able to find at the local grocery store such as green and pink peppercorns, dried cilantro, powdered jalapeño pepper, and hot paprika. A real treasure trove for spice lovers!

Mo Hotta Mo Betta
P.O. Box 4136
San Luis Obispo, CA 93403
(800) 462-3220 (nationwide)
(805) 544-4051 (in CA)

Husband and wife owners Tim and Wendy Eidson call themselves hot and spicy gourmet extraordinaires, and their 15-page catalog is mail order nirvana if you're the kind of person who enjoys foods with a bite. Notable low-calorie selections that I've used to spice up steamed vegetables include Cajun Garlic Sauce, Jalapeño Mustard, and Vinagré Picante, a blend of rice vinegar, chilies, garlic, tomatillos, and black pepper.

Pendery's
304 E. Belknap Street
Fort Worth, TX 76102
(800) 533-1870

This is the mailing list to be on if you want to try malagueta pepper, a variety with just a hint of ginger and cardamon, or highly aromatic nonya seasoning from Malaysia or a Tunisian meat seasoning called tabil. Pendery's also carries specialty gourmet gadgets such as tortilla presses, grain grinders, and fajita pans.

G.B. Ratto & Company
821 Washington Street
Oakland, CA 94607
(800) 325-3483 (nationwide)
(800) 228-3515 (in CA)

A treasure-house of ethnic foods, Ratto's lets you choose among such unusual spice blends as berbere, a hot Ethiopian spice blend, and zather, a mixture of ground sumac and ground thyme that can be moistened with a touch of olive oil and slathered on diet bread for an authentic Mid-Eastern treat. My favorite spice is the powdered jalapeño peppers—a pinch can lend any dish a touch of Mexican magic. Ratto's also offers a marvelous selection of vinegars in hard-to-find flavors such as pear and orange sherry.

San Francisco Herb Company
250 14th Street
San Francisco, CA 94103
(800) 227-4530

A free encyclopedic 32-page catalog full of tempting herbs and spices is available on request.

Santa Fe School of Cooking Catalog
116 W. San Francisco Street
Upper Level Plaza Mercado
Santa Fe, NM 87501
(505) 983-4511

For an all-star lineup of fresh and dried chilies, this is the catalog to get. Grind several varieties together and make them into a chili powder that is so rich and fresh it will make you swoon. Their small catalog is especially strong on unusual chilies like guajillo, with its earthy flavor and fruity aroma, and pasilla, a purple-black chili with an intense smoky flavor.

Seaside Banana Garden
6823 Santa Barbara Avenue
La Conchita, CA 93001
(805) 643-4061

Although Seaside is not a spice purveyor, I thought I'd include them here because bananas are the ultimate diet aid—low in calories, filling, and sweet. This is my favorite source for exotic bananas from all over the world. Call Seaside for prices on a 5½-lb. sampler pack of assorted varieties, all labeled so you get a "banana education" while you're enjoying their products.

Simpson & Vail
P.O. Box 309
Pleasantville, NY 10570
(800) 282-TEAS or
(914) 747-1336

For soothing or invigorating teas, as well as many imported spices and condiments, pastas, beans, and tea-related gifts, this is a venerable name that's been around since 1929. Especially strong on fruit-flavored decaffeinated teas such as apricot, kiwi/watermelon, red currant, mango, chocolate mint, and passion fruit.

Spectacular Sauces
P.O. Box 30010
Alexandria, VA 22310
(800) 999-4949

Every unusual sauce, condiment, and salad dressing you could possibly imagine is listed in this exceptional, free catalog. Many are low in calories and fat and provide an easy way to liven up foods without spending any time in the kitchen. Especially noteworthy: Santa Fe Exotic's Pineapple Salsa; Nervous Nellie's Sweet Jalapeño Sauce, and Sengthongs' Thai Tamarind Dipping Sauce.

The Spice Merchant
P.O. Box 524
Jackson Hole, WY 83001
(307) 733-7811

This is my secret source for every Chinese, Japanese, Thai, Indonesian, and Vietnamese condiment ever invented, including the wasabi and dashi listed as ingredients in the "Japanese Spice Blends" section. Be sure to try owner Dave Bigge's special Sri Lanka Curry Kit for only $4.50, with its pre-measured whole spices that you roast and grind yourself to make a deliciously unusual curry powder.

Spices Etc.
P.O. Box 5448
Charlottesville, VA 22905
(800) 827-6373

This is a first-rate, comprehensive resource for exotic chili blends, chunky dried vegetable flakes like dried carrot and potato dices, and natural French flavoring essences like cassis and lime that can jazz up any low-fat dessert. There's even a mustard lover's gift pack and the entire repertoire of Sweet Heat marinated seasonings, including Caribbean, Szechuan, Curry, Rio Grande, Sicilian, and Mediterranean. Spices Etc. doesn't just stop there—they whip up their own unique spice blends like Virginia Seafood Blend and Cinnamon Toast Popcorn Seasoning. A large line of spice grinders rounds out the assortment of great stuff. The catalog costs $2.

Sultan's Delight
P.O. Box 253
Staten Island, NY 10314
(800) 852-5046 or
(718) 720-1557

Middle Eastern food has a flavor palette all its own, and Sultan's Delight is a complete resource for Arabic, Syrian, Persian, and Turkish spices. Some of the more unusual offerings include mixed Syrian spices, dried ground lemons from Iran, and crystallized vanilla.

Variety Spices
P.O. Box 277
Lithonia, GA 30058

Variety Spices specializes in out-of-the-ordinary spices and offers most of the unusual kinds mentioned in *Skinny Spices*. Their catalog costs $1, which is refundable on your first purchase.

Watkins
150 Liberty Street
Winona, MN 55987
(800) 533-8018

These are the famous flavor extract people, with varieties that taste sinful (like caramel and butter rum) but are just 1 or 2 calories per capful. Blend them into yogurt with a little sweetener or into ricotta cheese for a delightful taste treat.

Wax Orchards
22744 Wax Orchards Road, SW
Vashon, WA 98070
(800) 634-6132 or
(206) 463-9735

Wax Orchards is the salvation of dieters everywhere, with its incredible fruit-sweetened fudge sauces that weigh in at just 16 calories per teaspoon. Great drizzled over fruit, these sauces are available in Fudge Sweet Original, Amaretto, Orange Passion, and Peppermint. Their fruit-sweetened preserves at only 7 calories per teaspoon are wonderful, too.

Wild Weeds: A Catalogue of Herbal Delights
P.O. Box 88
Redway, CA 95560
(707) 943-3835

A New Age catalog, Wild Weeds carries everything from organically grown culinary herbs to edible flowers. Many of the varieties can also be used for medicinal purposes or in teas as part of homeopathic remedies.

Wooden Spoon
P.O. Box 931
Clinton, CT 06413-0931
(800) 431-2207

In addition to all kinds of spice racks, including the attractive wooden wall-mount variety, Wooden Spoon features Select Origin Tri-Color Pepper, a Yogurt Cheese Funnel that makes creating yogurt cream cheese a snap, and intensely flavored Orange and Lemon Cooking Oils that add fabulous flavor without a lot of fat.

23.
MORE SPICY READING

T he following books were helpful in preparing *Skinny Spices* and inspirational in terms of my own weight loss.

Light & Spicy by Barbara Gibbons; Harper & Row, 1989. $10.95. "The Slim Gourmet" does it again with the most mouthwatering collection of spicy recipes anywhere. A true delight whether you're just browsing through, preparing a recipe, or sampling the delicious results.

The Nutri-System Flavor Set-Point Weight-Loss Cookbook by Susan S. Schiffman and Joan Scobey, with recipes by Robin Rifkin; Little, Brown, 1990. $18.95. You don't have to participate in the Nutri-System Program to benefit from this excellent combination of recipes and thought-provoking insights about dieting.

Chopstix by Hugh Carpenter and Terry Sandison; Stewart, Tabori & Chang, 1990. $29.95. A fun collection of low-fat, spicy recipes inspired by the enticing flavors of Asian and Mexican cuisine. **Chopstix** deliciously combines a cookbook, travel memoir, and visual tour of the Los Angeles contemporary art scene.

Microwave Gourmet Healthstyle Cookbook by Barbara Kafka; William Morrow & Co., 1989. $22.95. Great for dieters who want their food in a hurry and appreciate imaginative cooking with spices and herbs.

The Calorie Factor: The Dieter's Companion by Margo Feiden; Simon & Schuster, 1989. $29.95. A truly encyclopedic guide to calorie, fat, and carbohydrate listings for more than 250,000 foods. This is the only book I've ever found that even lists calorie counts for various types of sushi.

Delicious Diet Cookbook: The Sensible Way to Slim by Lois Levine; Macmillan Publishing, 1974. $6.95. Unfortunately, out of print, but a treasure trove of easy-to-fix low-cal goodies, with lots of good suggestions for enhancing food with the magic of herbs and spices.

Totally Hot: The Ultimate Hot Pepper Cookbook by Goodwin, Perry, and Wise; Dolphin/Doubleday, 1986. $12.95. Everything in this flame-red book is understandably hot and spicy, with many recipes for dieters who want to "go for the burn"—on their tongues, that is. This fine book is also out of print, but your local library may have a copy.

365 Diet Tips by Julie Davis; Ballantine Books, 1985. $3.50. A one-tip-a-day book filled with great advice for strengthening your resolve in the face of overwhelming temptation. Especially good as a source for developing moderate eating behaviors.

Diet Center It's a Natural Cookbook compiled by Sybil Ferguson; 1976. $3.00. Available only to Diet Center clients, this cookbook is filled with extremely low-calorie recipes that taste terrific. Try to borrow a copy from a program member, or look for one at a garage sale.

Sophie Kay's Yogurt Cookery by Sophie Kay; HP Books, 1978. $4.95. A healthy collection of yogurt-based recipes that even non-yogurt lovers will enjoy.

New Gourmet Recipes for Dieters by Francine Prince, Simon & Schuster, 1981. $8.95. Fantastic heart-healthy recipes such as Banana Raisin Bars and Pink Panther Potatoes help keep dieters on track.

How to Lose Weight and Enjoy It by Lillian Dee and Marty Wolfson; Wolfson Publishing Co., 1972. $2.95. So old that it may actually qualify as an antique, this book touts a specific weight-loss program developed by the authors. Nevertheless, it contains some wonderful recipes (especially for salad dressings, dips, and desserts) that contain few or no calories.

The Free and Equal® Dessert Cookbook by Carole Krupa; Surrey Books, 1992. $9.95. All of Carol's books are marvelous, including this one, filled with easy-to-prepare recipes for sweets and desserts made with Equal® brand sugar substitute instead of sugar. Her companion volume, **The Free and Equal® Cookbook,** focuses on appetizers and main dishes made with Equal.® Both books are also ideal for diabetics.

Eating Well by Burt Wolf; Doubleday, 1992. $20.00. My favorite TV chef, Burt combines low-fat recipes, culinary history, and celebrity anecdotes in his inimitable *bon vivant* style. A truly joyous and often hilarious cookbook.

INDEX

Spice blend families are given in boldface; recipes are shown in italic.

W, Y, Z